Elvio Lunghi

THE BASILICA OF
ST. FRANCIS
IN ASSISI

D1209317

SCALA/RIVERSIDE

© 1996 SCALA, Istituto Fotografico Editoriale,
Antella (Florence)
Layout: Anthony Mathews
Translation: Christopher Evans
Editing: Marilena Vecchi
Photographic acknowledgements: SCALA ARCHIVE
(M. Falsini, M. Sarri) except for: pp. 8, 9, 13 (G. Barone); pp.
51 and 131 (E. Ciol); p. 67 (F. Todini)
Printed in Italy by Arti Grafiche "Stampa Nazionale", Calenzano
(Florence), 1996

Front cover: Giotto, St. Francis receiving the Stigmata, detail
Back cover: Giotto, The Dream of Innocent III, detail

Published by Riverside Book Company, Inc.
250 West 57th Street
New York, N.Y. 10107
ISBN 1-878351-51-6

Contents

Brother Francis

"Francis was a native of Assisi, in the Spoleto valley. He was born (1182) during his father's absence, and his mother gave him the name Giovanni; but, on his father's return from his journey to France, he started to call his son Francis. As a young man, with a lively intelligence, he began to practice his father's profession, dealing in cloth, but in a completely different manner. Francis was far more cheerful and generous: he liked to enjoy himself and to sing, strolling around Assisi day and night with a band of friends, spending all the money that he earned or could get hold of on parties and entertainments.... One day, as he was walking past the church of San Damiano, he was moved to enter. Inside, he started to pray fervently in front of the image of the Crucifix, which spoke to him with touching kindness: 'Francis, can you not see that my house is falling down? Go then and repair it for me.' Trembling and amazed, the young man replied: 'I will do so willingly, Lord.'" (*Legend of the Three Companions*, I, 2)

Francis understood Christ's request literally, and took money from his purse to give to the priest who looked after the church, to pay for a lamp and oil so that there would always be a light under the sacred image. Shortly afterward, the merchant's son left his father's house and embarked on the life of a "penitent"; wearing a hermit's robe, he devoted himself to the repair of small decrepit churches, a practice that was very common at the time. He wandered through the streets of the city begging for the stones he needed to do this work. He used to say: "Whoever gives me one stone will have one reward; whoever gives me two, two rewards, whoever three, the same number of rewards." After repairing the church of San Damiano, where he was later to take the young Clare, Francis continued his life as a penitent in the humble chapel of Santa Maria della Porziuncola. This was a rural dependency of the abbey of San Benedetto al Subasio. Francis completed its restoration three years after his conversion.

"But one day, while listening to Mass, he heard the instructions given by Christ when he sent out his disciples to preach: that is to take nothing for their journey, neither gold, nor silver, neither bread, nor staves; neither footwear, nor a change of clothing. He understood these orders better afterward, when he had got the priest to explain the

passage to him: Then, radiant with joy, he exclaimed: 'It is exactly what I long to do with all my strength!' " (*Legend of the Three Companions*, VIII, 25)

Casting off his hermit's clothes, he made himself a tunic out of coarse fabric, cut in the shape of a cross, girdled at the waist with a piece of rope, and began to preach the Gospel in a simple manner. He was soon joined at the Porziuncola by his first companions, drawn by a way of life based on poverty, chastity, and obedience to the Church, in the manner of the Gospel. Francis decided to call them "Friars Minor." As the community grew, Francis went to Rome to obtain the papal *placet*. At the time the Church was engaged in harsh repression of the heretical beliefs widespread among lay people and had forbidden the formation of new religious orders outside the rule of St Benedict. Nonetheless Pope Innocent III authorized Francis to preach his penitence. Having obtained approval from the pope, the movement grew with marvelous speed and the novelty of its way of life impressed Bishop Jacques de Vitry, who visited Perugia in 1216:

"I have found though, in those regions, something that has been a great consolation to me: people, of both sexes, wealthy and lay, who, stripping themselves of all property for Christ, abandoned the world. They were called *frati minori* and *sorelle minori* and are held in great esteem by the pope and cardinals.

"They do not meddle at all in temporal matters, but instead, with ardent desire and passionate commitment, labor everyday to wrest foundering souls from the grip of worldly vanities and draw them into their ranks. And, by divine grace, they have already produced much fruit and many have gained by it, so that anyone who hears them tells others: come, and see with your own eyes.

"These people live in the manner of the early Church, of which it is written: 'the multitude of the faithful were of one heart and one soul' During the day they go into the towns and villages, striving actively to win others for the Lord." (Jacques de Vitry, *First letter*)

Francis died at the Porziuncola in the evening of October 3, 1226. For two years he had borne the mysterious marks of the stigmata on his hands, feet, and side, which he had received on the mountain of La Verna after seeing a vision of a seraph. While he lived, the saint kept the scars carefully concealed, but they were revealed after his death by his best-loved disciple Elias, who had been a personal friend of Francis and his deputy from 1221 to 1227:

"And now I announce to you a great joy, an extraordinary miracle. Never has such a portent been heard of in the world, except in the Son of God, who is Christ the Lord. Some time before his death, our brother and father appeared to have been crucified, bearing the marks of the five wounds on his body, which were truly the stigmata of Christ. His hands and feet were pierced as if by nails passing from one to the other side, and had scars the black color of the nails. His side appeared to have been pierced by a spear, and often discharged drops of blood.

"While he lived he had a plain appearance and there was no beauty in his face: there was no member of his body that was not lacerated. His members were stiff, through contraction of the nerves, as happens in a dead body. But after his death his face became very beautiful, shining with wonderful purity and comforting to see. His members, rigid previously, became flexible and could be bent in any way one wished, like those of a tender child." (Letter written by Brother Elias)

The next morning a great crowd came down from Assisi, along with all the clergy, took up the sacred body, and carried it with great honor into the city, to the accompaniment of hymns, songs, and trumpet blasts. Passing by San Damiano, the procession halted for a while for a last farewell to Clare – founder of the Order of the Damianites – and, having at last reached its destination, the coffin was interred in the church of San Giorgio, just outside the old city walls, where the convent of St Clare (Santa Chiara) would later be built. Francis's tomb immediately became the object of intense popular devotion, stirred up by the news of the first miracles.

"Our Lord Pope Gregory [IX], having consulted the cardinals and numerous other prelates and approved the reports of the miracles worked by the Lord through Francis's intercession, inserted his name in the list of saints venerated by the

Church, ordering that the anniversary of his death be celebrated as his feast day.

"The ceremony of canonization was conducted in Assisi, in the presence of many dignitaries of the Church, a large group of princes and barons, and a countless multitude of people who flocked there from different places, and which the Pope had convened in the year of Our Lord 1228, the second of his pontificate." (*Legend of the Three Companions*, VIII, 71). By order of Gregory IX, the Franciscan Thomas of Celano wrote a biography of Francis, the *Vita prima* (1228). In 1246 Tommaso compiled a *Vita secunda*, drawing on the information he had gathered from the saint's first companions on the instructions of the minister-general, Crescenzio da Iesi, who was anxious to preserve the deeds and words of Francis. In 1260 the Chapter in Narbonne entrusted the new minister-general, Bonaventura da Bagnoregio, later St Bonaventura, with the task of writing a new biography. Called the *Legenda major*, it was presented at the following Chapter, held in Pisa in 1263. Three years later the General Chapter in Paris ordered the destruction of all biographies of the saint predating the *Legenda major*, which became the official interpretation of St Francis propagated by the Order. St Bonaventura did not confine himself to recounting the story of Francis's life, but presented him "in the guise of the angel who rises from the east and bears on himself the seal of the Living God, as described by that other friend of Christ, the apostle and evangelist John, in his accurate prediction. Indeed John says in *Revelation*, on the opening of the sixth seal: And I saw another angel ascending from the east, having the seal of the living God." This vision was based on the Joachimite interpretation of the historic role of St Francis that had been put forward by the more extreme fringes of the Spiritual Franciscans, faithful to the saint's last will dictated in his *Testament*.

The Construction of the Church

The process of Francis's canonization was not yet complete when negotiations got under way for the construction of a monumental church in his honor. The interested parties were the Church of Rome, anxious to bring a movement made up largely of lay people within the fold of the ecclesiastical institution; the Friars Minor, who wanted to celebrate their saintly founder in a fitting manner; and of course the city of Assisi, which aspired to become a place of pilgrimage. The site chosen was the western tip of the Asio hill, where it sloped steeply down to the valley of the Tescio river. The place had been used by the medieval city state for executions and for this reason was known as the "Hill of Hell." On March 29, 1228, Simone di Pucciarello donated to Brother Elias, who received it on behalf of Gregory IX, a site outside the walls on which to build a church that the friars could use to keep the body of St Francis. Exactly a month later, Gregory IX granted an indulgence of forty days to all those who contributed with donations and works to the construction of a "special church." Before ascending the papal throne, Ugolino da Ostia had held the post of cardinal protector of the Order of the Minorites, a position that had led to a long friendship with Francis. The pope was in Assisi throughout the month of May, engaged in the investigation that formed part of the process of Francis's canonization, which concluded on July 16 with a solemn concelebration. The following day Gregory IX personally laid the first stone of the new church.

"This Pope, who had loved Francis exceedingly when he was still alive, not only paid him great honor by enrolling him in the company of the Saints, but also had a church erected to his glory, laying the first stone himself, and then enriching it with sacred gifts and precious ornaments. Two years after his canonization, the body of St Francis, taken from the place where it had been interred earlier, was solemnly transferred to this new church.

"To it the pope sent the gift of a gold cross, gleaming with precious stones, on which a relic of the wood of Christ's cross was mounted. Along with this, decorative objects, liturgical furnishings and other objects to be used for serving at the altar, and many precious and splendid church vestments.

"The basilica was exempted from any jurisdiction lower than that of the pope and, by apostolic authority, proclaimed by him 'head and mother' of the whole order of Friars Minor, as attests the charter promulgated in a bull signed by all the cardinals." (*Legend of the Three Companions*, XVIII, 72)

On October 22, 1228, Gregory IX announced that the building under construction was subject to no authority but that of the Roman pontiff, who was the owner of the land on which the church was being erected. This ecclesiastic exemption was intended to avert potential conflicts with the local religious authorities in the future, and perhaps to placate criticism from the most zealous followers of Francis's legacy as well. In fact criticisms and claims from the latter were not slow to emerge, with the result that the pope was obliged to reaffirm the pontifical rights over the church less than two years later. In the meantime the work was proceeding quickly and on May 16, 1230, Gregory IX granted various indulgences to those who were involved in the transfer of the saint's body from San Giorgio to the new church. The solemn ceremony took place on the following May 25, in the presence of Minister-General Giovanni Parenti and a vast crowd. At this point a regrettable incident occurred: in order to thwart any attempt at seizure and to ensure that the city retained Francis's body in its entirety, the civil authorities of Assisi took possession of the sacred remains and, locking themselves inside the church, concealed them in the bowels of the earth beneath the high altar. This caused an enormous scandal and Gregory IX fiercely condemned what had

Above: Giotto, The Crib at Greccio, *detail. The detail shows part of the rood-screen that used to stand in the presbytery of the lower church and that, as was the custom in monastic churches, once separated the nave from the chancel of the friars.*

Below: the nave of the lower church. Following the model of Romanesque buildings in the region, the lower church was designed as a great crypt, with a single nave dug out of the rock.

happened, threatening the city with excommunication and the friars with revocation of the ecclesiastical exemption.

The ceremony of translation could be said to mark the conclusion of the first phase of construction, which comprised the area around the altar and the nave of the lower church. The building's unusual architectural form derives partly from the terrain on which it stands – the lower ridge of a steeply sloping hill – and partly from its function as a container for relics. The lower church is actually a gigantic crypt, with massive Romanesque forms perpetually steeped in semi-darkness and used for veneration of the saint buried under the high altar. It has a plan in the form of a Tau cross, a symbol dear to Francis. The original design was for a single nave divided into four bays with quadripartite rib vaults, ending in an apse with a hemispherical vault facing to the east and with a short transept roofed with a barrel vault. The work started from the presbytery, which is set right on top of the living rock, while a deep cut had to be made into the side of the mountain to build the nave. The interior was lit by narrow single-light windows in the middle of each bay – filled in when the chapels were built – as well as in the vault of the apse and the walls of the transept. Light also entered the latter through the doors linking it to the monastery, accessible by means of two staircases. The atrium at the entrance, where the ribs of the vault have a different profile from those of the nave, was added later, though at

a time prior to the completion of the upper church. Access to the tomb was blocked by a rood-screen – an architectural structure that can still be seen in Franciscan churches north of the Alps, such as the Franziskanerkirche at Rothenburg ob der Tauber in Franconia – that separated the part of the church open to women from the shrine itself. It served as a screen for pilgrims and was necessary to the liturgy, as mass was celebrated from an altar set on top of a pulpitum. One like it is depicted in the *Crib at Greccio* (XIII) of Giotto's *Legend of Francis*, an episode set close to an altar underneath a ciborium – in reality a tabernacle like the one that still exists in Santa Chiara. Behind it can be seen a rood-screen with a door, through which several women are peering, with a crucifix leaning in toward the nave set above it. Some fragments of this rood-screen, consisting of slabs of marble decorated with mosaics, have been re-utilized in the parapet of the singing gallery of St Stanislas and in the chapel of the Magdalen.

The upper church has the appearance of a large and brightly lit Gothic hall, divided into four bays with a transept and polygonal apse. The marble throne set in the middle of the apse is a reminder that it was originally intended for use as a papal chapel, while the continuity of space between the chancel and the nave simplifies its function as a hall for preaching to the people. The bays are roofed with quadripartite vaults, supported by shafts that extend down to the ground as slender clustered piers. About a third of the way up, the walls are set back to form a passage that runs all the way round the church, passing behind the piers and, in the transept, underneath a triforium. The vast hall is illuminated by the rose window in the facade wall and large windows set in the clerestory – the upper part of the walls – which let in enough light for the scenes frescoed on the walls to be clearly visible. As one approaches the altar the light level increases, streaming in through two large four-light windows set at the ends of the transept and the enormous windows that have entirely replaced the walls of the apse. These techniques are characteristic of contemporary French Gothic architecture; They are quite exceptional for the Italian architecture of the time and can only be explained by the direct intervention of builders from the other side of the Alps. The same may be said of the crocket capitals of the piers. On the outside the thrusts of the vaults are countered by cylindrical buttresses set against the walls, against which rest flying buttresses. The facade has a very simple appearance that is reminiscent of the cathedral of Assisi and the tradition of Romanesque churches in the region, in particular the rose window surrounded by symbols of the Evangelists and the animal figures on the string course. The double portal with its pointed arches, characteristic of churches of pilgrimage,

and its stylized leaves on the capitals, is a rare homage to Gothic culture from across the Alps. The gigantic campanile, once topped by a steeple, was erected after the upper church had been completed.

Nevertheless there are considerable differences between the upper church and the great Gothic cathedrals of the Paris region. This is seen both in its more modest dimensions, resulting from the choice of a single nave, and in the extreme simplicity of the architectural members. The interior is largely covered with pictorial decorations, producing an effect that is even more austere than that of the buildings constructed by the Cistercians around the same time. The impression created is one of a building erected in a great hurry, on the crest of the wave of popular feeling that followed the death and canonization of the Poor Man of Assisi.

If the decision to dedicate a church-cum-monumental reliquary to Francis of Assisi was taken by Gregory IX, who claimed its direct ownership on more than one occasion, Franciscan tradition holds Brother Elias of Beviglie to have been materially responsible for the work, the man whose tenacity made possible the completion of the construction. Appointed minister-general in 1232, Elias went to great lengths to raise the necessary funds, sending visitators to all the provinces of the Order. His authoritarian methods provoked a great deal of ill feeling, leading to open rebellion in 1239, followed by his removal from the post.

In 1235 Gregory IX was in Assisi again, where the large numbers of people that turned up for the occasion obliged him to celebrate Mass on a portable altar in the open air. By the following year the upper church was already complete in its essential lines and a monumental *Crucifix* was hung from the beam set at the end of the nave, with a tiny portrait of Brother Elias weeping at Christ's feet. Further evidence that the work was finished while Brother Elias was still the minister-general is provided by the date 1239 that used to be inscribed on the bells of the campanile, along with the names of Elias, Pope Gregory IX, and Emperor Frederick Hohenstaufen. The construction of the church was favored by a long truce in the dispute between the Empire and Papacy, represented visually by the scaly eagles, symbol of the Counts of Segni from whom Gregory IX was descended, set on the west front and at the base of the piers on the inside of the facade, and the presence of a crowned bust carved on the impost of the four-light window in the south transept, which has been identified as a portrait of Emperor Frederick II Hohenstaufen. In 1236 the latter had sent a letter to Elias describing the solemn burial of his cousin St Elizabeth of Hungary in the church in Marburg that had been dedicated to her. The widow of the Landgrave of Thuringia, she had become a Franciscan Tertiary and had been canonized in Perugia by Gregory IX in 1235. An altar in the

The facade of the upper church. Very simple in shape and with modest sculptural ornamentation, the facade is based on the model of the Romanesque cathedrals in the Spoleto valley. The only concession to the new Gothic style of architecture from across the Alps is the double portal under a pointed arch which was characteristic of places of pilgrimage.

north transept of the lower church would be dedicated to her. This would explain the presence of Frederick's portrait on the outside of the transept, which could not have been placed there after the fall of Elias. In December 1239 Elias went to meet Frederick II in Pisa even though the emperor had been excommunicated by Gregory IX the previous April, and for this reason the pope excommunicated the friar as well.

Over the following years the struggle between the Roman pontiff and the excommunicated emperor intensified. On two occasions Frederick threatened Assisi itself with his troops, and each time it was saved from sack by the miraculous intervention of St Clare. On the death of Gregory IX (in 1241) the throne of Peter remained vacant for two years. The new pope, Innocent IV, left the peninsula for a long exile in Lyons, which came to an end only with the death of Frederick II (in 1250). Returning to Italy, Innocent IV settled in Perugia, where he remained for two years. On April 27, 1253, the pope came to Assisi and on the following May consecrated the altars and church of San Francesco in the presence of a vast crowd.

View of the apse from the fifteenth-century cloister. This reveals the coherence of the original design, with its two superimposed stories, the lower one convex in plan and the upper polygonal. The face of the wall, completed without any interruptions, is built entirely of white and pink limestone from Subasio, except for the blocks of ancient travertine that reinforce the corners of the transept.

The portal of the lower church. Carved shortly after the year 1300, at the end of the program of renovation of the crypt, this magnificent portal is the work of the same local craftsmen who were responsible for the capitals of the chapels and of the Cerchi monument located in the atrium behind.

The First Painted Images

It is apparent from the first glance that the church of San Francesco is an extraordinary showcase of paintings. In fact it contains the most complete mural decoration of the thirteenth and fourteenth century to be found in Italy. Nor is there any example elsewhere in Europe that is comparable in the richness of its imagery. And yet for many decades the walls of the two churches, especially the upper one, presented a bare and austere appearance, accentuated by the almost total absence of sculptural reliefs. This was particularly true of the main facade, the place where the religious imagination of the Christian West was usually exercised in the age that we call Gothic. On the most solemn feast days, it was the altars alone that were loaded with splendors, covered with cloth of gold and precious ornaments. There is a story about a certain Fra Ginepro who, from the vantage-point of an altar above the rood-screen, was set to guard a valuable antependium made of cloth of gold draped over the altar on Christmas Day of 1230. The Treasury of the Convent still has two beautiful altar frontals of embroidered silk that were donated by John of Brienne, King of Constantinople, to adorn the altar during the ceremony of the transfer of St Francis's body.

The first image placed in the church was probably the *Crucifix* that Brother Elias had had painted for the upper church in 1236, where he is shown in adoration at the feet of the martyr, with an inscription alongside revealing his identity: "Frater Helias fieri fecit. Iesu Christe pie miserere precantis Helie. Iuncta Pisanus me pinxit A.D. MCCXXXVI". St Francis was particularly devoted to the symbol of the Cross. His biographer St Bonaventura tells us that he used to urge his companions to concentrate their attention on an image of Christ Crucified, identifying themselves with his passion, as a substitute for books in which to read the Office, which were in short supply.

The *Crucifix* that spoke to St Francis in the small church of San Damiano is still preserved with loving care in the church of Santa Chiara. Here Christ is depicted according to the Romanesque iconography of the *Christus triumphans*, i.e. portrayed alive enthroned on the cross. The *Crucifix* painted by Giunta Pisano, on the other hand, follows the Byzantine iconography of the *Christus patiens*, that is with the dead Christ bent sorrowfully on the cross, as in the *Crucifix* painted by the same artist for the shrine of the Porziuncola. This iconographic type, developed in the Byzantine East, was introduced into the West at the time of the first crusades and appeared in painting and goldwork to the north of the Alps in the middle of the twelfth century. It is likely that the iconographic model was suggested to the painter by Brother Elias himself, who for three years had been in charge of the Minorite province of the Holy Land and had undoubtedly had the opportunity to see sacred images of a highly devotional character in the Holy Sepulcher. This prototype was to provide the inspiration for numerous *Crucifixes* painted in the thirteenth century for the Franciscan communities of the peninsula. In the flood of sacred images produced in the first two centuries of the basilica's existence, Giunta Pisano's *Crucifix* is the only one to be clearly marked with the name of the artist, a sign of the great esteem in which the Pisan artist was held. Some time later, he was also commissioned to paint the *Crucifix* for the church of San Domenico in Bologna, where the founder of the other great mendicant order of medieval Europe was buried: St Dominic de Guzman. Giunta's *Crucifix* remained on display in the upper church until the seventeenth century, on a beam supported by two corbels that can still be seen on the walls of the nave. Some idea of its original location is conveyed by a scene in Giotto's *Legend of Francis*, the *Verification*

16

Page 16: Giotto, Verification of the Stigmata, *detail.*

Above: "Master of the Treasury," Saint Francis and Four of his Miracles, *Treasury of the Convent. An old picture painted shortly before the consecration of the church, in 1253. The four miracles at the sides illustrated the saint's wonder-working powers to pilgrims.*

Below: altar frontal of embroidered silk, Treasury of the Convent. Made in Palermo, it was donated to the Assisi church by John of Brienne at the time of the solemn transfer of St Francis's body, in 1230.

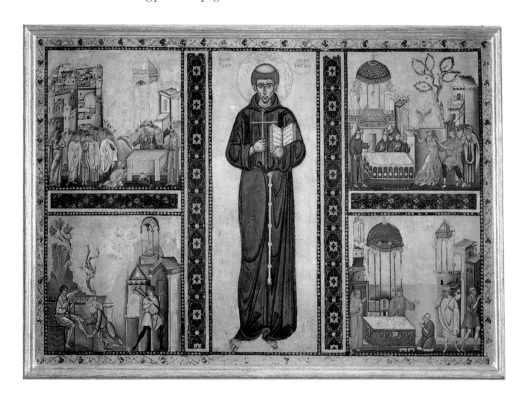

of the Stigmata at the Porziuncola (XXII). This is set in the nave of a church crossed by a beam supported on corbels, on which stand a Crucifix between a painted Madonna and a sculpted St Michael.

Along with Brother Elias's *Crucifix,* others were set on the church's altars and used for everyday liturgical functions. One can be seen from behind above a rood-screen in the fresco of the *Crib in Greccio* (XIII). The representation is so realistic – showing in detail the wooden structure and the tripod used to fix the object to the wall – that it seems likely that the painter was accurately depicting the situation on the rood-screen of the lower church. Two more *Crucifixes* based on the model of the *Christus patiens* also come from San Francesco: one is in the Treasury of the Convent and the other in Cologne Museum, where it was taken in 1836 by the German painter J.A. Ramboux. They were painted by an anonymous artist active in the Franciscan communities of Umbria, the Marche, and Emilia around the middle of the thirteenth century, known to scholars by the name of the "Master of the Blue Crucifixes" owing to his habit of painting the clothes worn by his figures in a bright blue. Although they are fairly small in size, around one meter high, the structural work excludes their having been used as processional crosses. The two crosses must have been visible from both sides, as the figure of Christ is painted on each face. Thus they were placed on detached altars rather than on altars set against a wall. The most credible hypothesis is that they were located alongside or hung above the main altars of the two churches, the only ones that can be viewed from both sides, at a date not long after the solemn ceremony of consecration carried out by Innocent IV in 1253.

The Treasury of the Convent contains an important altar frontal depicting *St Francis and Four of his Miracles.* Portraits of the saint appear in large numbers in churches founded by communities of Minorites in the province of Umbria and Tuscany immediately after Francis's death. The oldest painting that we know of bears the date 1228, the year of his canonization. These altarpieces, inspired by Byzantine hagiographic icons but adapted so that they could be placed above an altar, were usually vertical and pointed at the top. An image of the saint giving his blessing was set in the middle and scenes from his life and of his miracles at the sides. The altarpiece in the Treasury differs in its horizontal form and its exclusive concentration on the miracles of his canonization, including one that took place at the first tomb in the church of San Giorgio – the miracle of the little girl with her head stuck to her shoulder – and two at the altar in the lower church – the miracle of the cripple Niccolò from Foligno and the miracle of the girl from Norcia possessed by a devil. The protagonist of the fourth miracle – St Francis healing the cripple Bartolomeo from Narni – is a poor pilgrim. The possibility that the painting was set on top of the altar-reliquary or placed against its front in the manner of an *antependium* can be excluded. It was probably set above or in front of the aforementioned rood-screen that separated the area accessible to lay people from the sanctuary reserved for priests and friars, where the miraculous events had taken place. This also explains the unusual iconography of the image of St Francis, which shows him with the stigmata clearly visible on his hands and feet, holding a cross, and displaying a book in which the rule of his life is written: "If you wish to be perfect, go and sell all that you have and give it to the poor." In March of 1237, Pope Gregory IX made a determined attack on those who denied the existence of the stigmata, declaring that it was no sin "if so singular a privilege, to the greater

Giunta Pisano, Crucifix, *Museum of the basilica of Santa Maria degli Angeli. It is a reproduction of the one, now lost, that Brother Elias had had painted for the church of Assisi, in which he was portrayed praying at Christ's feet.*

"Master of the Blue Crucifixes," Crucifix, *Treasury of the Convent. There is an identical image of "Christus patiens" on each side of the Crucifix. The cross was set in an isolated position, above the main altar or at the end of the nave, so that it could be seen both by the friars in the chancel and the worshippers in the nave.*

glory of Him who has granted it, be made visible to the eyes of devotees through the testimony of painting." This situation seems to be reflected in the panel in the Treasury, where the presence of the stigmata does not take priority over the thaumaturgical purpose of the painting. The choice of the episodes shows that the saint's cult, in the years immediately following his death, was based exclusively on extolling the miraculous properties assigned to his mortal remains, invoked by the pilgrims who flocked to his tomb and made known by Thomas of Celano in his *Trattato dei miracoli.* This important painting is part of a complex figurative phenomenon known as the "lingua franca," which involved artists of various nationalities, but particularly Venetians, working for the crusader kingdoms of Palestine and Cyprus following the Fourth Crusade of 1204, which led to the foundation of

the Latin kingdom of Constantinople. Crusader artists frescoed an apse of the Kalenderhane Camii in Constantinople with scenes from St Francis's life at a date prior to 1261, the year that the city was re-conquered by Michael Paleologus. Among the Latin Kings of Constantinople, an eminent role was played by John of Brienne, who met Francis under the walls of Damietta and was present in Assisi for the canonization of the saint. His daughter Yolanda married the German Emperor Frederick II Hohenstaufen, bringing him the title of King of Jerusalem as a dowry. On John of Brienne's death in 1237, his body was brought to Assisi and was buried in the lower church, to which he had donated precious gifts when alive. It is in this context that we should see the image of St Francis preserved in the Treasury.

The Fresco Decoration
of the Lower Church

Innocent IV spent the whole of the spring and summer of 1253 in the Convent. Noting that the much revered church was not yet finished in a fitting way, on July 10 he authorized Fra Filippo da Campello, the procurator of the basilica (an administrative post created in 1240 to get round the prohibition on the handling of money), to spend the alms given by the faithful for the next twenty-five years on the completion of the construction and on its decoration with noble works. In this he was following the instructions of Rinaldo da Segni, the Cardinal responsible for the Order, in contravention of its Constitutions and against the wishes of the minister-general and the friars of Assisi. A few days later the pope gave permission for the friars to accept books, chalices, crosses, and other objects made of gold or silver for use in the church, as well as precious church vestments, which were on no account to be alienated. Having celebrated the feast day of St Francis on October 4, Innocent IV moved to Anagni and from there went on to Naples, where he died in December 1254. Within a few days Rinaldo da Segni was elected pope and assumed the name of Alexander IV. He was the nephew of Gregory IX, who had made him responsible for the Minorites in 1227, a post that Alexander IV did not wish to give up to anyone else. As a Cardinal Rinaldo had made great efforts on behalf of the Order. As pontiff (1254-61) he would leave an indelible mark on the church in Assisi, having the lower church lined with frescoes and installing stained-glass windows in the upper church.

The program for the decoration of the lower church took its inspiration from a spiritual interpretation of St Francis that Alexander IV had made his own. Present at the saint's death, he had seen and touched the wounds discovered on his body, in particular the bleeding hole in

his side. In a letter written by the pope in October 1255, the Poor Man of Assisi was described almost as if he were a second Christ – an expression taken up by St Bonaventura in his *Legenda major* – who bore the signs of the redemption of humanity worked by the Savior Jesus on his mortal body. On the walls of the nave five episodes from the life of St Francis, set on the south side, are paralleled by the same number of episodes from the Passion of Christ, on the north side. The sequence commences from the bay adjoining the narthex and finishes at the point where the rood-screen was placed: I) *Christ laying his Clothes at the Foot of the Cross – Francis renouncing his Father's Inheritance*; II) *Christ on the Cross entrusting Mary to John – Innocent III dreaming that Francis is holding up the Crumbling Church of Rome*; III) *The Deposition of Christ from the Cross – Francis preaching to the Animals*; IV) *The Lament over the Dead Christ – Francis receiving the Stigmata from a Seraph*; V) *Christ is Recognized by the Disciples at Emmaus – The Discovery of the Stigmata on St Francis's Body*.

The iconography of the stigmata received by Francis with the apparition of a seraph follows the account given in Thomas of Celano's *Vita secunda* (1247), from which one of the *tituli* that accompany the scenes is taken. In the *Legenda major*, on the contrary, St Bonaventura declared that it was the Crucified Christ who appeared to Francis on Mount La Verna in the guise of a seraph. This means that the frescoes were certainly painted before 1263, the date that the *Legenda major* was finished.

It was the clients' intention that the pictorial decoration should accompany the path of the pilgrim from the entrance to the saint's tomb, overlaying the architectural framework of the church-reliquary and emphasizing its funerary symbolism. On the ceiling, which is painted

Page 20: "St Francis Master," Francis preaching to the Animals, *detail.*

Oblique view of the nave of the lower church. Though it was damaged by the opening of the chapels, the nave retains large sections of mural decoration carried out shortly after 1253.

with a starry sky alluding to the Kingdom of Heaven, the artist set tiny mirrors in the plaster to strengthen the illusory effect. The symbolic figure of the star reappears in the inlaid work of the floor and in the altar in the form of a sarcophagus.

Although damaged by the holes knocked in the walls and the loss of large areas where the paintings had been completed in tempera, these frescoes mark the beginning of an important chapter in thirteenth-century Italian painting, characterized by the meeting of the Byzantine tradition and the new Gothic forms. Much of the decoration was painted by the "St Francis Master," an anonymous artist who takes his name from an icon depicting the saint in the sanctuary of the Porziuncola. The various works carried out by this master in churches outside Assisi and the influence he exercised on Umbrian painting are evidence for his local origin. He was probably a friar resident in the Convent of Assisi, where there must have been a workshop specializing in the production of devotional images, especially Crucifixes, needed by the community of Minorites. The length of his stay in Assisi brought him into contact with craftsmen from the other side of the Alps who were working on the decoration of the windows in the upper basilica. He himself provided designs for stained-glass windows and it was from this practice that he derived his predilection for lines that were elastic and flowing, although not yet fully Gothic. Alongside the "St Francis Master," the work of the "Master of the Blue Crucifixes" is also apparent in these frescoes. His contribution is recognizable by the characteristic blue color of Christ's loincloth in the *Scenes of the Passion.*

The "St Francis Master" also worked on the walls of the sanctuary, where a few fragments can be seen. The same painter also frescoed the isolated figure of the *Virgin and Child with an Angel* on the right-hand wall of the fourth bay above the tomb of Cardinal Pietro di Barro, who died in Assisi in October 1252 and was buried at this point in the church. This is the first tomb of a prelate from outside the Order that we know about, and was placed there in defiance of the ruling of the Constitutions of Narbonne that burial in churches belonging to the Friars Minor should be reserved for the members of the Order.

"St Francis Master," Scenes from the Passion of Christ and Saint Francis. *The frescoes set five episodes from the Passion of Christ next to the same number of scenes from the life of St Francis, which are the oldest of the wall paintings devoted to the saint.*

In the pictures: Francis preaching to the Animals, Christ on the Cross entrusting Mary to John, The Lamentation over the Dead Christ, *and* The Deposition of Christ from the Cross.

The Stained-Glass Windows
of the Upper Church

During the papacy of Alexander IV, Minister-General Bonaventura da Bagnoregio presented a series of rules governing the internal life of the Order to the chapter of friars that met in Narbonne in 1260. Among the sections devoted to the observance of poverty comes a prohibition on the use of masonry vaults in churches, except in the main chapel, and an excessive amount of decoration with paintings, sculptures, windows, and columns; the length, width, and height of churches should conform to the local custom. The only ornamentation permitted was the use of large figured windows in the chancel behind the high altar, where stained-glass windows depicting Christ on the Cross, the Virgin Mary, and Saints John, Francis, and Anthony could be installed.

The status of the church at Assisi as an Apostolic See rendered it exempt from internal regulations intended to curb excesses, but the need to put a stop to the mania for ever grander and more splendid constructions could no longer be postponed, as is apparent from Thomas of Eccleston's account of the settlement of Friars Minor in England. However it is significant that the ban did not extend to icons with the image of St Francis, particularly common on the Italian peninsula, or to the use of figured glass, typical of Gothic architecture north of the Alps. Examples predating the Chapter of Narbonne can be seen in the chancel of the Elisabethskirche in Marburg (Hessen) and in the church of the Discalced at Erfurt (Thuringia).

Like the clerestory of a Gothic cathedral, the upper church was created to house what was the first set of figured stained-glass windows in Italy, and is still the largest. The problem of the lack of any tradition in the production of stained glass was overcome at Assisi by bringing in craftsmen from across the Alps to set up furnaces for the fusion and staining of glass, establishing a link with the builders of the great Gothic cathedrals and Franciscan churches of Northern Europe. This acted as a conduit down which artists, iconographic ideas, and formal solutions flowed.

Notwithstanding the clumsy restorations and extensive alterations, the unitary nature of the program is still apparent. It started, as soon as the construction was complete, with the three two-light windows in the chancel, where the life of

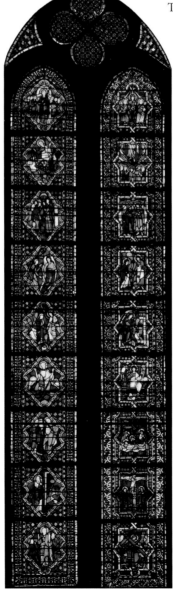

Christ is represented – childhood, public ministry, and Passion – accompanied by scenes from the Old Testament, according to the principle of typological concordance between the Old and New Testaments that was a firmly established part of scholastic teaching. The artist who made these stained-glass windows came from a classical figural culture, inspired by Byzantine iconography, that was typical of miniatures and of goldwork in the central regions of Germany during the first quarter of the thirteenth century. There is a very close link with the windows depicting the life of St Francis in the church of the Discalced at Erfurt, which permits us to date the execution of the windows in Assisi to the years 1235-50, before the church's consecration in 1253 and in all likelihood during the papacy of Gregory IX, when Brother Elias was still minister-general.

There is a considerable stylistic difference between the stained-glass windows in the choir and the ones in the transept and nave, on which work began at the time of Alexander IV: it was under his pontificate that Clare of Assisi, who figures among the Virgins in the south four-light window, was canonized (1255). The windows in the nave represent a complete apostolic cycle, following a model that was extremely widespread in the cathedrals of Northern Europe. It is probably no accident that St Peter and St Paul are missing in the windows, their places taken by St Francis and St Anthony of Padua, here given the rank of apostles for their activity as preachers. Peter and Paul have an altar dedicated to them in the north transept, which Cimabue was to fresco with scenes from the life of the princes of the apostles, founders of the Church of Rome. The Roman stamp on the basilica of Assisi is set by the two tondi on the inside of the facade depicting busts of Peter and Paul.

The stained-glass windows were made by two main craftsmen. In the four-light window in the south transept, depicting Genesis and the *Ordo Virginum,* and the two apostolic windows in the nave – the ones with Saints James the Greater, Andrew, John, and Thomas – it is figurative designs of French origin that prevail, which have features in common with the style of Gothic *rayonnant* introduced into the

Parisian miniature during the reign of King Louis IX, St Louis, around the middle of the thirteenth century. This monarch was particularly devoted to St Francis, wore the habit of the Third Order, and sent precious gifts to the basilica of Assisi, including a splendid missal for use on the altar of the lower church that had been illuminated in a Parisian workshop around 1255-56. The stained-glass windows in Assisi bear a close resemblance to the ones depicting the apostles in Tours Cathedral.

The four-light window in the north transept, with the appearances of Christ up to the Ascension, and the windows in the nave representing the apostles Bartholomew and Matthew and Saints Francis and Anthony of Padua are the work of the "St Francis Master," whom we have already met on the walls of the lower church. The master's Umbrian workshop was also responsible for the first two windows on the wall to the left of the entrance, one depicting six angels and the Glorification of St Francis carried at Christ's breast as the Christ Child is carried by the Virgin in the lancet alongside – an iconography drawn from St Bonaventura's *Legenda major* – and the other with figures of prophets and bishops. The last two stained-glass windows on the south wall, representing the apostles Simon and Thaddaeus and Philip and James the Less, are almost entirely the product of modern restorations.

The Beginning of the Pictorial Decoration
of the Upper Church

In the upper church, the higher part of the north transept has a pictorial decoration with many parts missing and altered, that forms part of a figural program predating the involvement of Cimabue. Unlike the work of the "St Francis Master" in the lower church – where the scenes from the lives of Christ and Francis use the walls merely as a medium, without any *trompe-l'oeil* perspective – these frescoes are perfectly integrated with the architectural lines of the church, using the painting to make up for its lack of decoration compared to the prototypes north of the Alps. Their iconography and composition were designed to fit in closely with the stained-glass windows, so as to create the illusion of a continuous transparent surface. Not only is there a window in the wall at the end of the transept, but it also looks as if this wall is pierced by the niches painted with images of the Prophets Isaiah and David, which echo the outline of the architectural moldings surrounding the panes of stained glass in the real window. The gestures of the two prophets allude to the Ascension set at the top of the four-light window and deepen its significance. The design for the window was made by the "St Francis Master," whereas the murals have been identified as the work of a "Master from beyond the Mountains," also a designer of stained glass and figuratively linked to the French workshop responsible for the southern four-light window.

The transalpine training of this artist is apparent in the pointed Gothic gables painted on the outside of the triforium, inspired by the Gothic *rayonnant* style of architecture, while the statuesque effect sought in the figures of the apostles, six on each side, painted against the back wall of the triforium, displays affinities with the gallery of personages on the inner facade of Reims Cathedral. In the two scenes frescoed in the side lunettes, forceful in their expressiveness and enlivened by vibrant linear effects, depicting the *Transfiguration* and the *Eternal Enthroned with the Symbols of the Evangelists* in an allusion to *Revelation*, iconographic links with French and English miniatures have been detected. The decoration of the north transept was executed during the pontificate of Clement IV (1265-68), whose coat of arms representing a lily is repeated along the archivolts.

Salimbene da Parma tells us that the Archbishop of Narbonne did not want to assume the papacy until he had visited the church of San Francesco in Assisi. It was during his pontificate that the long conflict between the Church of Rome and Emperor Frederick II and his heir Manfred was brought to an end. In an attempt to drive the hated Swabians out of the Kingdom of Sicily, his predecessor Urban IV (1261-64) had asked for help from the French king, St Louis, and on the latter's refusal, from his younger brother Charles of Anjou, offering him the title of Roman senator. With the election of Clement IV, King Charles finally decided to invade Italy. By the May of 1265 he was in Rome at the head of an army and on February 26, 1266, routed Manfred's Swabian army at Benevento, clearing the way for the Angevin conquest of the kingdom and the victory of the Guelph Communes over their Ghibelline rivals. By a strange coincidence, just a month later Clement IV authorized the procurator of the church Piccardo di Angelo, St Francis's nephew, to extend for three years the privilege granted by Innocent IV in 1253, which had allowed the offerings of the faithful to be used for the decoration of the church. It is likely that Clement IV had the walls of the upper church decorated in gratitude for the successful outcome of the war against the Swabians and set out to reproduce the appearance of a northern French cathedral by means of fictive painted architecture.

The "Master from beyond the Mountains" also started to fresco the vault of the chancel, where his bright violet tones and stylized plant decorations copied from the repertory of English manuscripts can still be seen on the ribs, but for some unexplained reason – perhaps the unavoidable halt caused by the activity of the Chapter General, which met in Assisi in 1269 – the Gothic workshop was released from its obligations and its place taken, some time later, by that of Cimabue. The choice of the Florentine painter meant a reversal of the preferences for the Gothic world of Northern Europe that had long been dominant in Assisi and a shift toward the classical revival that had been taking place in Roman art ever since the election of Pope Nicholas III Orsini (1277-80), himself of Roman origin.

View of the north transept. This is where the pictorial decoration of the upper church commenced, carried out by a "Master from beyond the Mountains", Gothic by training and probably of French origin. The frescoes, now hard to decipher as is evident from the detail (St Paul) on page 26, are superimposed on the architectural lines of the building. The decision to fresco the church in its entirety was taken by Clement IV, whose coat of arms, a lily, is set repeatedly along the archivolts of the walls.

Cimabue at Assisi

A valuable *terminus ante quem* for the resumption of work on the decoration of the presbytery walls is suggested by a detail, invisible to the naked eye, located on the vault above the altar. The cross vault is occupied by the Evangelists, each seated on a wooden throne while he writes the Gospel and flanked by his symbol – the Man, the Lion, the Ox, and the Eagle. In front of each Evangelist is the region of the world for which he is traditionally supposed to have written his Gospel: Judea for Matthew, Italy for Mark, Greece for Luke, and Asia for John. *Ytalia* is represented by a simplified view of Rome, squeezed within the Aurelian walls and with seven or eight clearly visible landmarks, apparently copied from life and most of them easily recognizable: the Senatorial Palace, the Basilica of St Peter's, the Torre Milizia, the Pantheon, the *Meta Romuli*, and Castel Sant'Angelo. The Senatorial Palace is distin-

guished by several large coats of arms of the Orsini family and the Roman Senate (S.P.Q.R.). These armorial bearings can still be seen on the ceilings of the Palace on the Capitol and date from a precise historic event, the time when, on the expiry of Charles of Anjou's mandate as Roman senator (September 1278), the newly elected Pope Nicholas III Orsini personally assumed the post, appointing his brother Matteo Rosso as vicar. On the death of Nicholas III (in 1280), the conclave held in Viterbo appointed Simon de Brion as his successor: a French prelate with close ties to the Angevins, he took the name of Martin IV. Charles of Anjou assumed the senatorial title again, this time for life. The Orsini coats of arms painted in the vaulting cell representing St Mark fix the date of the frescoes to some time between 1278 and 1280, during the pontificate of Nicholas III. Unlike the emblems of Clement IV in the north transept, they are an indication not of the pope's direct involvement in the undertaking, but of the historical context in which the work was carried out.

Before ascending the papal throne and since 1261, Giovanni Gaetano Orsini had been the cardinal responsible for the Minorites, a post he retained until 1279 when, at the request of the friars, who had put forward the name of their general Girolamo da Ascoli, he had himself replaced by his favorite nephew Matteo Rosso. The bull *Exit qui seminat* of August 1279 represents an unanswer-

able defense of the ideals of St Francis against the excesses of the Spirituals and the opposition of the secular clergy, as well as a definitive integration of the Order into the institution of the Church. The Church became the legitimate owner of the buildings occupied by the friars, who retained the right to their use. Nicholas III was also responsible for the adoption of the Franciscan breviary into the Roman liturgy. The celebration of the supremacy of the Church, extolled by the pope in the frescoes of the *Sancta Sanctorum* in the Lateran, forms the basis of the iconographic program adopted in the upper church of Assisi, dominated by the pontifical throne. It takes its inspiration from the dedication of the three altars to the Virgin, the apostles, and St Michael the Archangel, and the choice of the episodes depicted is an interpretation of their respective feast days. The scenes from the life of the Virgin in the apsidal tribune are meant to signify the Church generated by Mary; the scenes from the lives of the apostles in the north transept allude to the founders of the Church of Rome. The Apocalypse in the south transept refers to the coming of the Kingdom of God with the affirmation of the dominion of the Church over society. Behind the altars are painted two large Crucifixions, based on successive episodes in the Gospel according to John and presented for adoration by the friars singing in the choir. The artist called on to realize this grandiose program was the Florentine painter Cimabue, whose presence in Rome in 1272 must have made him aware of the liking for antiquity displayed by Nicholas III, a descendant of one of the most illustrious of Roman families. This liking of his is clearly represented by the frescoes in the *Sancta Sanctorum*, personally commissioned by the pope, and was shared by the Florentine artist, as can be seen from the evolution that took place in his style between the early *Crucifix* in Arezzo and the one in Santa Croce. The frescoes in Assisi are the Tuscan painter's greatest work and certainly one of the highest creations, if not the highest, of Italian painting before Giotto. The reputation of the magnificent cycle is not limited to its political significance and its treatment of the religious questions of the day: the true reason for its fame lies in the extraordinary quality of the representations, in which Cimabue set him-

self up as the champion of the renaissance in Italy which took its inspiration from Constantinople, after the fall of the Latin Kingdom, but was already clearing the way for Gothic realism by subjecting traditional iconographies to a new dramatic imagination. This culminates in the tragic pathos of the *Crucifixion* in the south transept, surrounded by the restrained sorrow of Mary, who is clasping John's hand, the desperate scream of Mary Magdalene, the soft singing of the choir, the tumult of the heavenly spheres, and the tiny figure of Francis embracing the wood of the cross. Giorgio Vasari, who was able to see the frescoes before their colors faded, commented: "This truly great work by Cimabue, so richly and skillfully executed, must in my opinion have astounded everyone at that time, especially as the art of painting had been completely unenlightened for so long. As for me, when I set eyes on it again in 1563 I thought it wonderfully beautiful and I was astonished at the vision that Cimabue had

Cimabue, The Virgin taking Leave of the Apostles. *This episode is the first in the story of the life and glorification of the Virgin, to which the lower half of the apsidal tribune is devoted. On the upper part of the walls are set the events preceding the* Annunciation, *from the* Announcement to Joachim *to the* Marriage of the Virgin.

shown, although he was surrounded by so many shadows." It is our misfortune that this imposing group of paintings should have come down to us in a very poor state of preservation due to oxidation of the white lead. Extensively employed by the painter, the pigment has turned black and caused a general darkening of the paint, producing an effect similar to that of a photographic negative.

Cimabue took from the "Master from beyond the Mountains" the device of setting the sacred drama inside an illusionistic work of architecture, but chose to replace the *rayonnant* style of architecture with more sober forms drawn from Tuscan Romanesque or from Early Christian buildings. Rows of depressed arches on slender fluted columns with Corinthian capitals and mosaic tiles on the front, half-length figures in polygonal marble frames, painted corbels that appear to hold up coffered cornices, bright plant friezes spilling out of cantheri supported by telamones with their heads hidden in the vegetation, flat moldings studded with red crosses: altogether, these

Cimabue, The Death of the Virgin. *Monumental composition with a strong emotional impact, in which the arrangement of the figures, set in a dialectical relationship with the painted architecture, creates the illusion of a three-dimensional space. The inspiration came from early Christian mosaics, studied by Cimabue during his stay in Rome (1272). The cycle's precarious state of preservation prevents us, today, from appreciating the solemn classicism that made Cimabue the champion of Byzantine painting, contrasted by Dante with the "modern" painting of Giotto.*

motifs constructed a homogeneous decorative framework that was intended to give a realistic appearance to the figured scenes, producing an effect of monumental grandeur that had not been seen in the West since the fall of the civilizations of antiquity. The same repertory would be systematically adopted in the whole of the upper church by the various artists involved in the enterprise, creating the organic and unitary result that the friars of Assisi were looking for.

Examining the iconographic program of the decoration, we find that the whole of the tribune is given over to a celebration of the Virgin Mary. The festivals of the Immaculate Conception and the Visitation were introduced by the General Chapter that met in Pisa in 1225, but it was the next Chapter held in Assisi in 1269 that laid particular emphasis on the worship of Mary, by requiring all the friars present free from other obligations to celebrate a Mass in her honor. The requirement to hold such a Mass every Saturday was then extended to the whole community. The frescoes in the lunettes at the sides of

the three-light window depict the Life of the Virgin: the *Announcement to Joachim, Joachim's Offering at the Temple,* the *Nativity of the Virgin,* and the *Marriage of the Virgin.* Under the gallery, the story of the Virgin after the death of Christ is related: from the left, the *Virgin taking Leave of the Apostles,* the *Death of the Virgin,* the *Virgin's Soul being received by Christ,* and the *Assumption to the Throne of Christ in Heaven.* The decoration of the south

transept is devoted to angels, a very common subject in Romanesque art because of its eschatological implications. In fact the altar is dedicated to St Michael the Archangel. Full- or half-length figures of angels are depicted in large numbers, while the western lunette contains *Three Archangels defeating the Beast of the Apocalypse.* Scenes from the Revelation of St John run along the wall underneath the gallery, starting from the altar, where

Cimabue, Christ and the Virgin Enthroned. *This is one of Cimabue's most extraordinary inventions and one of the greatest masterpieces of medieval painting. Christ is represented in the act of blessing a group of Friars Minor kneeling at the foot of his throne, where they have been invited by the Virgin who intercedes for them. Francis's devotion to the Mother of God was passed on intact to his followers.*

there is a fresco of the *Crucifixion:* the *Vision of the Throne and the Book of the Seven Seals,* the *Vision of the Angels at the Four Corners of the Earth,* the *Apocalyptic Christ,* the *Fall of Babylon,* and the *Angel showing John the New Jerusalem.* The decoration of the north transept is devoted to the apostles Peter and Paul and is a replica of the frescoes that used to be in the atrium of St Peter's in the Vatican. The scenes run in a clockwise direction, again starting from the tribune: *St Peter healing the Cripple, St Peter healing the Sick and driving out Devils,* the *Fall of Simon Magus,* the *Martyrdom of St Peter,* and the *Martyrdom of St Paul;* the *Crucifixion* appears again above the altar.

Cimabue, The Vision of the Throne and the Book of the Seven Seals. *This is the first episode of the cycle of the Apocalypse depicted by the artist in the south transept. The iconography adopted differs from previous Western representations of the Last Judgment – which set Christ the Judge at the top* surrounded by the apostles and patriarchs, paradise in the middle, and the resurrection of the dead and hell at the bottom – but follows the description in the Roman missal for the feast day of St Michael the Archangel, to whom the altar is dedicated.

Cimabue, The Vision of the Angels at the Four Corners of the Earth. *The scene, based on the text of the Revelation of St John, depicts four angels against the background of a battlemented city, holding back the winds that come from the four corners of the earth. Above, and now virtually indecipherable, the Vision of the Angel with the Seal of the Living God.*

Cimabue, Apocalyptic Christ. *The vision of the throne of God surrounded by seven angels with trumpets and of the angel burning incense before the altar takes place in the presence of the multitude of the elect, many of whom wear the habit of the Friars Minor. The themes of the Apocalypse were the subject of much debate within the order, which claimed that some of the interpretations of Gioacchino da Fiore referred to the Franciscans, but this view encountered opposition from the Church. In 1279 Nicholas III condemned the abuses of the most zealous followers of Gioacchino and integrated the order definitively within the institution of the Church.*

Cimabue, The Fall of Babylon. *At the words of the angel flying in the midst of heaven, the buildings collapse while unclean spirits and strange birds flee from the wide-open gates of the city. This is one of the most fantastic of Cimabue's paintings,* *with its tumultuous vision of the buildings opening up like a pack of cards in a Cubist composition and the surrealistic little theater of animals in the foreground.*

Above: Cimabue, Saint John and the Angel. *The scenes from Revelation end with the angel showing John the New Jerusalem. The very poor state of preservation of these frescoes is due to the loss of large areas of the finishing "a secco" and the oxidation of the white lead.*

Below: Cimabue, Saint Peter healing the Cripple. *This is the first of five scenes from the life of the apostles Peter and Paul, to which the lower part of the north transept is devoted. Two of them, taken from the* Acts of the Apostles, *depict miraculous acts of healing carried out by St Peter.*

Cimabue, Saint Peter healing the Sick and driving out Devils. *The subject of these frescoes complements the apostolic cycle in the stained-glass windows of the nave, in which Francis of Assisi and Anthony of Padua occupy positions corresponding to Peter and Paul. It is likely that the altar in the transept was dedicated to the apostles and the saints, in homage to the two patron saints of the Church of Rome.*

Page 40, above: Cimabue, The Fall of Simon Magus. *The episode, described in the apocryphal "Acts of Saint Peter" and Jacobus de Voragine's "Legenda Aurea", formed part of the scenes from the life of the apostles that used to decorate the porch of the old Vatican basilica, now known to us only through seventeenth-century drawings.*

Page 40, below: Martyrdom of Saint Peter. *The scene, in which the architecture plays a primary role, is set between two monuments of ancient Rome: the pyramid of Caius Cestius (on the left) and the "Meta Romuli" (on the right).*

Cimabue, Martyrdom of Saint Paul.

Page 42: Cimabue, Crucifixion *in the south transept (above);* Crucifixion *in the north transept (below). Of these two monumental Crucifixions, the first is perhaps the most tragic representation of the Passion of Christ in medieval Western art and depicts the moment, preceding his death, in which Christ entrusts Mary to his favorite disciple John. The other represents the moment just after Christ's death, with the soldier piercing his side with a spear and the swooning of Mary. St Francis appears in both, embracing the wood of the cross.*

Page 44: *view of the vault of the north transept of the lower church.*

The First Alterations in the Lower Church

A *Madonna with the Divine Child* giving his blessing is painted on the east wall of the north transept. She is seated on a wooden throne supported by four angels. On her left – to the right from an observer's viewpoint – stands a barefooted St Francis holding a closed book. It is possible that there used to be another saint on the right of the Virgin, or the painting may have simply been interrupted by the window that let light into the transept, with its embrasure decorated with frescoes by the "St Francis Master." The window is visible in the passage leading to the chapel of the Maddalena, which must have been symmetrical with the opening in the opposite wall. Beneath the *Maestà* five beatified Franciscans are depicted in adoration, set above an altar. This altar is not recorded as being dedicated to the Immaculate Conception until after 1476, at the time of the Franciscan pontiff Sixtus IV,

but it is likely that it had been dedicated to the Virgin Mary ever since the closing decades of the thirteenth century. It was at this time that devotion to the Mother of Christ became extremely popular within the Order, to judge by the large number of altarpieces depicting the Virgin that are to be found in Franciscan churches, eclipsing the earlier popularity of portraits of St Francis. The existence of such an important prototype in the mother church in Assisi could hardly have been ignored. Although it has been extensively repainted, the attribution of the *Maestà* to Cimabue has never been questioned. The five blessed Franciscans, on the other hand, are the work of Pietro Lorenzetti. Cimabue's fresco was spared during the fourteenth-century renovation of the decoration of the transept for a reason that we can only guess at today: the heart-rending beauty of the work, an

46

Page 45: Cimabue, Maestà. *The Madonna and Child, seated on a throne borne up to heaven by angels, was frescoed on the altar dedicated to the Virgin, located in the north transept, alongside the saint's tomb. It is to this tomb that the celebrated portrait of St Francis in the right-hand margin of the panel alludes.*

Page 46: Rubeus (?), funeral monument to John of Brienn. The work is located in the atrium of the lower church and was carved in the closing decades of the thirteenth century by an artist of Northern European Gothic culture, probably the same Rubeus who worked on the Fontana Maggiore in Perugia (1277).

absolute masterpiece of thirteenth-century Italian painting and a prototype imitated by the greatest artists of the time, such as Duccio di Buoninsegna in his *Rucellai Madonna*. No less moving is the portrait of the saint, more faithful than any other to the description of Francis made by his first biographer Thomas of Celano.

An examination of wills made in Assisi in the second half of the thirteenth century shows just how rooted was the desire to be buried alongside the tomb of St Francis. Even a pope, Martin IV, expressed the wish to be buried in Assisi. However, since death took the pope while he was in Perugia, in 1285, the people of that city refused to give up his mortal remains to their hated rival Assisi and prepared an honorable tomb for him in their own Cathedral.

It was during the pontificate of Martin IV (1281-85) that the great sepulchral monument to an Emperor of Constantinople set against the wall opposite the nave was built. It consists of a very tall Gothic aedicule supported by two small pillars in the *rayonnant* style. The base is adorned with coats of arms bearing the cross of Jerusalem and statuettes of apostles. Two angels pull aside the drapes of the mortuary chapel, revealing the dead body lying on a bed. Above it are set two asymmetrical groups: on the right a *Virgin and Child*; on the left a crowned male figure – a portrait of the deceased – seated with his legs crossed in the manner of the rulers of France, on a faldstool supported by a marching lion. The personage represented is probably John of Brienne, King

of Constantinople and Emperor of Jerusalem, a personal friend of St Francis and benefactor of the basilica of Assisi who was buried in the lower church. His tomb was recorded in the list of burials compiled by the sacristan Galeotto in 1509. Emperor John was highly venerated by the Minorites: in 1452 Benozzo Gozzoli portrayed him at Montefalco wearing the Franciscan habit and it is in this guise that he appeared in the choir stalls of the upper church made by Domenico Indivini (1501).

The monument's disjointed appearance is explained by the fact that it was originally set against a different wall of the church. It was moved to its present site, where it covers a thirteenth-century decoration, following the breaking down of the walls for the construction of the minor chapels and the demolition of the rood-screen at the end of the nave. In the absence of documentation, any hypothesis as to its sculptor must be based on style, which is reminiscent of the lively Gothic gestures used on a bronze lintel above the door of the bishop's palace in Orvieto Cathedral (*circa* 1290) that bears the signature of Rubeus. The same artist also made the bronze basin of the Fontana Maggiore in Perugia (1277) and modeled the large bronze statues of the *Griffin* and the *Lion* in the same city's Palazzo dei Priori (1274). All these sculptures appear to be the work of a notable master, probably of transalpine origin, who had emerged from the lively international circle that gathered around the Papal Curia in the second half of the thirteenth century, in which French prelates played a prominent part.

The Nave of the Upper Church

It is legitimate to ask whether or not the iconographic program drawn up under the pontificate of Nicholas III envisaged an extension of the decoration to the walls of the upper church, and therefore whether Cimabue, when he left Assisi for Florence where the dome of San Giovanni was being lined with mosaics, appointed trusted collaborators in his place. It seems, on the contrary, that work on the decoration was interrupted for several years. The papal privilege that allowed the procurator of the Convent to use the alms collected in the church for the decoration of the building, granted by Innocent IV in 1253 for a period of twenty-five years and extended for a further three years by Clement IV in 1266, lapsed in 1281. Martin IV and Honorius IV did not confirm the privilege, perhaps partly owing to the difficult situation within the Order. But in February 1288, after a tough conclave, the former general of the Minorites Gerolamo Masci from Ascoli was elected pope, the first Franciscan to ascend the throne of Peter. He took the name of Nicholas IV in homage to Nicholas III Orsini, who had appointed him a cardinal. Only two days after his consecration, Nicholas IV sent numerous sacred vestments in various colors, silver vases, and a sum of money to the church in Assisi. On April 30 he informed the provincial minister and custodian of San Francesco that a ban had been placed on any religious order, of either sex, whether mendicant or not, acquiring or constructing churches, oratories, monasteries, or other sacred places in the city or its immediate surroundings; this was done in order to encourage the flow of alms for the support of the Convent. On May 14 the pope confirmed the privilege that had been granted to the friars of Assisi to say mass under interdict. The following day he enjoined the minister-general, the provincial minister, and the custodian of San Francesco to keep the money offered by the faithful at the altars of San Francesco and Santa Maria della Porziuncola, and to spend it exclusively on the maintenance and ornamentation of the Assisi church and the sustenance of the friars. The reason for this was that the city of Assisi was too small and did not provide a sufficient income to meet the needs of the religious community. It would be difficult to overestimate the consequences of these measures on the architectural development of Assisi, whose growth would be limited to the monastic complexes of San Francesco and Santa Chiara at opposite ends of the city, and on the material appearance

of the Order's mother church, with no limits placed on expenditure for its enlargement and maintenance.

During the years of his papacy (1288-92), Nicholas IV remembered with gratitude the time he had spent in Assisi in the past and, wishing to increase the flow of pilgrims to the saint's tomb, granted the church numerous indulgences to speed up the conclusion of the work under way. He personally sent precious gifts: among other things, a cloth for the altar of the lower church, embroidered with an image of St Francis in gold and ornamented with innumerable pearls and precious stones, which vanished at the time of the Napoleonic occupation. The Treasury of the Convent still contains a splendid chalice of silver gilt, bearing the name of the pope and the signature of the goldsmith Guccio di Mannaia from Siena. This is a work of extraordinary importance owing to the use of translucent enamel – the oldest known example of this technique south of the Alps – and to the knowledge of the most recent developments in the Gothic art of Paris displayed by the Sienese goldsmith, who showed himself to be an immediate forerunner of the art of Duccio, Simone Martini, and Pietro Lorenzetti. The pope himself must have been aware of the chalice's beauty and asked for his own portrait to be set among the figures of saints on its stem.

It is reasonable to suppose that the work dearest to Nicholas IV was the continuation of the iconographic program for the upper church. Unlike the frescoes in the transept, marked with the coats of arms of Clement IV and Nicholas III, the nave has neither coats of arms nor signatures and, if we exclude the date 1296 scratched into the painted plaster at the height of the gallery in the passage between the nave and the north transept, there are no objective clues as to when the work began. The only practical help is offered by modern art history, which has recognized the unmistakable style of Jacopo Torriti in the frescoes above the gallery behind the crossing. Torriti was the Franciscan painter whom Nicholas IV chose for the mosaic decoration of the apsidal tribunes of San Giovanni in Laterano (1291) and Santa Maria Maggiore (1296) in Rome. The frescoes in Assisi are earlier than the Roman mosaics, as is clear from their more old-fashioned approach to the representation of space, and the most likely date seems to be around 1288.

The decoration of the nave develops the theme of the

Left-hand bay of the nave and inside wall of the facade of the upper church. These two pictures clearly show the richness and complexity of the decorative program that covers the whole of the nave. Along the upper row run, in chronological order, the scenes from the Old and New Testament; along the lower row,

the scenes from the Life of Saint Francis. However the pictures can also be read vertically within each bay, establishing a direct link between the actions of St Francis and the example set by Christ and the patriarchs.

Below: Jacopo Torriti, vault of the Deesis; *right: "Isaac Master",* vault of the Doctors. *The two frescoed vaults of the nave sum up the iconographic program of the walls beneath. One celebrates the Church triumphant in the "tondi" depicting* Christ giving his Blessing, *the* Virgin Mary, *and* Saint Francis *and* Saint John *flanked by Angels; the other the Church militant, called on to prepare for the Kingdom of God on earth through the work of* Jerome, Ambrose, Gregory, *and* Augustine.

Jacopo Torriti, The Creation of the World. *This scene commences the biblical stories in the nave. From an iconographic point of view they are derived directly from the early Christian frescoes that could once be seen inside the Vatican basilica of old St Peter's. The influence of these Roman prototypes can also be recognized in almost all the medieval mural paintings of biblical subjects in the central regions of Italy.*

Jacopo Torriti, The Creation of Eve.

conformity of Francis's life to that of Christ, which was restricted in the lower church to a comparison between the salient episodes of the saint's biography and the Passion of Christ, extending it to the whole story of the Gospels and the book of Genesis. In the north clerestory are set episodes from the Old Testament, and, in the south, from the New Testament; the *Legend of Francis* is painted beneath the gallery on the lower part of the wall. The typology of St Francis – i.e. the search for models of morality in imitation of the life of Christ – is extended to the story of creation and the lives of the patriarchs. Identified by St Bonaventura with the angel of the sixth seal marked by the sign of the living God, the figure of St Francis became part of the story of salvation, in the expectation of the eighth day when, on the second coming of Christ, the dead will be resurrected and subjected to judgment. The key to the interpretation of the entire program lies in the oval pictures of the third cross-vault, where the saint is associated with the role of intermediary between God and humanity, reserved in the Bible for the Virgin Mary and the Baptist.

These motifs appear in three sermons on St Francis given by Matteo d'Acquasparta, preserved in manuscripts in the Assisi library and dating from around the same time as the frescoes. In the second sermon, in particular, devoted to the creation of man in the image of God, the great Franciscan man of culture uses analogies drawn from the figurative arts – pottery, sculpture, painting, engraving, ironwork – that show him to have had a deep understanding of the various arts, as is confirmed by his splendid cardinal's seal engraved by Guccio di Mannaia. It is my opinion, on the basis of the foregoing, that Matteo d'Acquasparta was responsible for the iconographic program of the nave. He was general of the Order from 1287 to 1289, and it was to him that Nicholas IV's famous letter authorizing the collection of money for the decoration was addressed. A lecturer at the University of Paris, he was the most faithful and consistent continuer of the line of thought followed by Bonaventura of Bagnoregio, from whose *Legenda major* are drawn the captions to the life of St Francis. Dante himself described him as the champion of the Conventuals against the Spirituals, represent-

ed by Ubertino da Casale. In other words, he was the main representative of the moderate tendency within the Order. Right to the end, Matteo lavished gifts on the Assisi church, to which, in 1287, he left half of his extremely well-stocked private library, along with various sacred vestments and pieces of goldwork, in accordance with a custom that linked him to the great benefactors of San Francesco, from Gregory IX to Robert of Anjou.

Turning to the decorative program, each bay of the clerestory is divided in two by a large window and comprises four scenes set on two levels. The sequence runs from west to east, first along the upper level and then, returning to the beginning, along the lower one. The scenes from the life of St Francis under the gallery take up only one row and should be read from west to east on the north wall, then the two scenes on the front wall, and finally from east to west along the south wall. The sequence has an obviously symbolic value. In the Christian conception of space and time, the orientation of a temple is not based on topography but on the divine scheme of history. In the Bonaventurian interpretation adopted by Matteo d'Acquasparta, St Francis is the angel ascending from the east, bearing the seal of the living God (*Revelation* VII, 2). His earthly existence follows a circular route, a symbol of perfection and of return to the Father.

The Old Testament, set on the north wall, begins on the upper level with the scenes of the Creation: *Creation of the World, Creation of Adam, Creation of Eve, The Fall, The Expulsion from Eden, The Labor of Adam and Eve, The Sacrifice of Cain and Abel,* and *Cain kills Abel.* The lower level is devoted to four Biblical Patriarchs, Noah, Abraham, Jacob, and Joseph: *The Construction of the Ark, Noah and the Animals entering the Ark, The Sacrifice of Isaac, The Visitation of the Angels to Abraham, Isaac blessing Jacob, Esau before Isaac, Joseph cast into the Pit by his Brethren,* and *Joseph makes Himself known to his Brethren in Egypt.*

The New Testament, located on the south wall, begins on the upper level with scenes from Christ's childhood: *Annunciation, Visitation, Adoration of the Magi, Presentation of Jesus in the Temple, Flight into Egypt, Dispute in the Temple,* and *Baptism of Jesus.* The lower row is devoted to the preaching of Christ and to his Passion: *The Marriage at Cana, Raising of Lazarus, Arrest of Jesus in the Garden, Christ before Pilate, Road to Calvary, Crucifixion, Lamentation over the Dead Christ,* and *The Holy Women at the Sepulcher.* On the inner wall of the facade are set the *Ascension of Christ* and a tondo depicting *St Peter,* to the south; the *Pentecost* and a tondo depicting *St Paul,* to the north.

The iconographic program is continued in the cross vaults, commencing with the *Four Evangelists* frescoed by Cimabue. The *Deesis* is depicted in the vault of the second bay from the transept: four tondi flanked by angels, alluding to the Kingdom of Heaven, contain *Jesus Christ giving his Blessing,* the *Virgin Mary* and *St John the Baptist* in the role of intercessors, and *St Francis alter Christus.* In the cross vault adjoining the facade are set the Four Doctors of the Church – clockwise, from the east: *St Jerome, St Ambrose, St Gregory,* and *St Augustine –* each intent on dictating his writings to a secretary. The remaining cross vaults are painted with a starry sky.

It is clear that such a complex undertaking could not have been completed in the four years of Nicholas IV's pontificate. It was painted by several artists in succession, on the basis of a preestablished program and under the strict supervision of the friars. The ornamental setting that encloses the individual scenes is the same throughout the church: it creates an illusionistic connection between the painting and architecture and masks the differences between the work of the various artists. The work of frescoing began from the clerestory of the bay adjacent to the crossing and was carried out bay by bay, with the

Above: Roman assistant of Jacopo Torriti, The Marriage at Cana.

Below: Roman assistant of the "Isaac Master," Pentecost.

ceiling being painted before the walls. In order not to block the nave completely and allow daily services to continue, the painter's scaffolds filled the space of one bay, from wall to wall and covering the area of the vaults, and were dismantled when that section of the decoration had been completed. Only after the upper part of the walls had been finished did work begin on the frescoes depicting the life of St Francis, starting from the second episode on the north wall and continuing in the direction in which they were to be read. The first scene in the cycle appears to have been the last to be painted.

The evolution of technology plays an important part in the story of the decoration. At a time when painting was still regarded as a mechanical art, Cimabue did not yet know how to use the technique of *buon fresco,* or true fresco, i.e. the application of earth pigments mixed with water onto fresh and still damp plaster, so that the liquid paint is absorbed by the surface and bonded to it by a chemical reaction, involving the crystallization of the lime mixed with sand as it combines with the carbon gases in the air. To achieve this result it is necessary for the painter to cover the *arriccio* – a preparatory layer required when the surface of the wall is uneven – with a thin layer of plaster that has to remain damp for as long as the painter is at work, and for this reason is known as a *giornata* ("day"). Cimabue did not paint in *buon fresco,* but on a wall that was already dry, with the final layer of plaster as large as the area covered by the scaffolding. In this case glue was mixed with the pigments to bond the paint to the plaster, a technique that did not produce such lasting results. The method of dividing the fresco into a number of *giornate* was first used in Assisi for the paintings in the nave. The detachment of some of the paintings, made possible by modern techniques of restoration, has revealed the *sinopia,* i.e. the preparatory drawing made on the *arriccio* and then covered by the final layer of plaster, which guided the painter in his work.

Giorgio Vasari thought that the whole upper part of the walls was painted in the characteristic manner of Cimabue and this view remained current until the time of Cavalcaselle, that is until the time when modern scholarship was applied to historical and artistic studies. The distinction of the work of different painters in the frescoes may appear irrelevant to some people, but is actually of considerable importance in that the decoration of the upper church in Assisi is the only work of art in Italy that presents us with a continuous picture of the transition from a Byzantine and immutable conception of sacred history, reflected in the imitation of God and still represented by Cimabue, to a Gothic and realistic vision that drew its inspiration from nature and whose champion was the Florentine painter Giotto. It was here in Assisi

Above: "Master of the Arrest," The Arrest of Christ.

Below: Giotto (?), The Ascension of Christ.

that Giotto "changed the art of painting from Greek to Latin, and ushered in the modern" (Cennino Cennini), but to bring about this transformation the contribution of two antagonistic schools of painting, the Florentine and the Roman, was required, and above all the maturation of a less pessimistic vision of earthly life that was in great part inspired by the love that St Francis felt for all creatures.

The iconography of the upper part of the nave is derived from cycles of paintings formerly in the Roman basilicas of St Peter's in the Vatican and San Paolo Fuori le Mura, but which have been lost. It is therefore natural that Roman painters were invited to ensure a faithful reproduction of the scenes. They were led by the Franciscan Jacopo Torriti, who personally frescoed the first two bays of the north wall, the *tondi* with the *Deesis* on the ceiling, and the upper row of the third bay with the *Expulsion from Paradise.* The scenes from the Gospels on the south wall are the product of a collaboration among independent masters – a practice very common in the workshops of the time if we are to credit the adventures of the Florentine painters Calandrino, Bruno, and Buffalmacco as related by Boccaccio. Dominant among them was an anonymous figure who has been given the name "Master of the Arrest." He collaborated with Torriti in the tondi of the ceiling and painted the scenes from the life of Christ in the second and third bay on his own. At this point Torriti was recalled to Rome by Nicholas IV, who entrusted him with the mosaic decoration of San Giovanni in Laterano, completed in 1291, and his place was taken by other artists who worked under the guidance of the very great painter of the two scenes of Isaac. The latter also intervened personally in the vault with the Doctors and left the task of finishing the decoration of the walls to close collaborators.

Although the choice of Torriti can be ascribed to the fact that he was a Friar Minor, his presence in Assisi, working on the most cosmopolitan structure in Italy, confirms that Rome had now become a major center of art, a meeting place between the spatiality of ancient painting, represented by the mosaics of the early Christian basilicas, and the dynamic and expressive capacities of Gothic design. This led to the emergence of a new kind of painting founded on an accurate three-dimensional representation of the reality of nature, expressed in plastic and monumental forms. The "Master of the Arrest" is a case apart. Trained alongside Cimabue, he collaborated with Torriti in the vault with the Saints and on the latter's departure took over the direction of the work, painting numerous scenes himself and collaborating with other artists in the scenes of the Passion and on the inside wall of the facade. In spite of fruitless attempts to identify his manner in Florentine or Roman paintings, the long time he

60

spent in the basilica suggests that he was a painter who got his training during the decoration of San Francesco, where he worked as an assistant to masters from outside until he earned himself a space of his own in the frescoing of the nave. This represents a continuation of the tradition of the workshop based in the Convent, which had supplied the other monasteries of the province with crucifixes and polyptychs at the time of the "St Francis Master." It is no accident that it had a particularly strong influence on Umbrian painters.

The shift toward a new classicism, based on rhythmically composed and strongly plastic forms, reached its peak in the two scenes of Isaac, where, for the first time in the Western world since the fall of pagan civilization, we find a concentration on significance and expression worthy of the masters of antiquity, as well as a conception of the painted surface as a concrete and measurable area, relying on the plastic quality of the images. On these walls we see a fusion of the compact mass of Arnolfo di Cambio's statuary, evoked by the Etruscan appearance of the figure of Isaac, and the practicable structures of Gothic imagery, a fusion that was to lead to a new naturalism, a synthesis of space and volume. The novelty of the solution could not have passed unobserved, and ever since the time of Thode (1885) the scenes of Isaac have been seen as the most original element in the whole of the decoration, a turning point that showed the way to the realism of the cycle of scenes from the life of St Francis below, and therefore the first manifestation of the art of the youthful Giotto, the Florentine painter to whom a well-established literary tradition, going back to a famous line of Dante's, gave the credit for having raised art to a new level at the end of the Middle Ages.

The Frescoes of the Legend of Francis

The grandiose iconographic program of the upper church reached its culmination in the twenty-eight panels devoted to the life of St Francis frescoed in the lower part of the nave. From the eleventh century onward it became a common practice in the West to paint isolated scenes from the life or miracles of a saint on the walls of the church containing his relics or where he was the subject of particular local devotion, but no attempt had been made to tell the complete story of a saint's life prior to Assisi. The frescoes of the *Legend of Francis* ushered in a new era in the application of the figurative arts to devotional purposes. The numerous copies that were made, in fresco or on panel, for the Franciscan churches of the neighboring regions were to confirm the special iconographic significance of the *Legend* – based on the official biography written by St Bonaventura – as a glorification of the saint who founded the Order, which gradually came to be ranked alongside the lives of Christ and the martyrs. Over the course of the fourteenth century its example was emulated in a large number of chapels and churches, especially in Italy, with cycles of frescoes devoted to the life and miracles of saints who had lived in recent times. The subject of popular devotion, some of these figures never got beyond the stage of beatification and did not obtain official recognition through a regular process of canonization. In the preface to the *Legenda major*, St Bonaventura explains the criteria he followed in writing his biography of St Francis:

"Besides, in order to avoid confusion, I have not always told the story in chronological order; I have endeavored rather to follow an arrangement that is better suited to bringing out the connections between the facts. For this reason I have felt it necessary to place things done in the same period of time under different headings, or to place things done in different periods under the same heading." The same criterion was followed by the deviser of the iconographic program, who did not wish the representation of the saint's life to be simply a series of episodes arranged in chronological order, but to present a continual and precise reference to the protagonists of the scenes from the Old and New Testaments painted on the upper part of the wall – regarded as types, i.e. as moral models for imitation – and thereby underline the complete accordance between the life of Francis and the life of Christ related in the Gospels.

To achieve this result, the walls are divided up by an illusionistic framework that represents a drastic departure from the solutions already used in the upper half of the nave. The width of each bay is taken up by three scenes, more or less square in shape. The lower part of the wall is covered with mock drapes, set underneath a heavy molding that appears to be supported by small projecting corbels. On this molding stand four spiral columns that hold up another coffered molding, decorated with mosaic tesserae. Above this are painted stone corbels that appear to support the gallery of masonry; they are represented at an angle, creating the illusion that they are converging on the central corbel, the only one that is depicted frontally, and producing a singular effect of perspective. The mock corbels painted by Cimabue, on the other hand, appeared to diverge from the center. The overall effect is that of an architraved portico, a sort of continuous stage that makes holes in the walls and allows the life of the saint to be seen set against the brightly-lit landscape of Umbria. The architectural framework also suggests the position of the observer, who should stand in the middle of each bay in order to understand the figurative message clearly.

When Hellenistic idolatry was supplanted by Christianity,

Page 62: Giotto, Clare taking Leave of the Saint's Remains in San Damiano *(XXIII), detail.*

Giotto, two triplets of the Legend of Francis. *The* Legend of Francis *was born from the collaboration between a great scholar and a very great painter. The former was responsible* *for the choice of the biographical episodes and their arrangement in a triadic pattern, following a rule of rhetoric. The painter was responsible for the invention of the illusionistic framework, composed of a portico on columns drawn in perspective, which adapts to the walls of the church a solution that was probably derived from the early Christian buildings of Rome.*

the new religion tolerated the presence of images in churches – notwithstanding the iconoclastic tradition of Judaism – while accentuating the spiritual element in the portraits of Christ and the saints. The attitudes of the figures, reduced in practice to stereotyped masks, were strongly conditioned by the liturgy and no attempt at anatomical accuracy or the imitation of nature was made. This approach is still evident in Cimabue's work in Assisi. In the first half of the thirteenth century, the admiration aroused by ancient sculpture, combined with a new interest in the appearance of natural phenomena inculcated by scholastic philosophy, produced the first signs of the renascence that was to come on the facades of the cathedrals of Chartres and Reims. Around the middle of the century, the "Master of the St Joseph of Reims" and the sculptors of the Sainte Chapelle in Paris added a more accentuated grace and lively gestures to the classical proportions. Statuary gradually freed itself from its role as a high-relief decoration applied to architecture and, growing in size and realism, transformed the portals of cathedrals into tableaux. This phenomenon reached a peak of illusionism in the beautiful western choir of Naumburg Cathedral (Germany), where the large figures of the Counts of Meissen, the founders of the church, stand as three-dimensional figures, relating to each other as individuals. On the Italian peninsula, the arrival of Gothic realism was announced by Frederick II Hohenstaufen, who proclaimed in his treatise on falconry that he wanted "to represent what exists as it is," and scattered portraits of himself in the guise of a Roman emperor throughout his kingdom. He found an enthusiastic follower in Giovanni Pisano, who built the facade of Siena Cathedral in the form of a theater thronged with monumental statues of prophets. The new style was slower to make an impression on painting, though, owing to the wave of Byzantinism that spread through Italy after the conquest of Constantinople during the Fourth Crusade (1204). The shift from an art based on the truth of Faith to an art founded on the imitation of nature took place in Assisi, on the walls of the church of San Francesco, where for the first time a brilliant painter set out to represent the life of a modern man, setting it in familiar places and trying to create an appearance of truth.

In fact the realism that we now impute to the use of theatrical devices received support from the early forms of religious drama, which developed in Umbria out of the singing of lauds by those in holy orders and by Minorite preaching. In his own sermons, St Francis was wont to

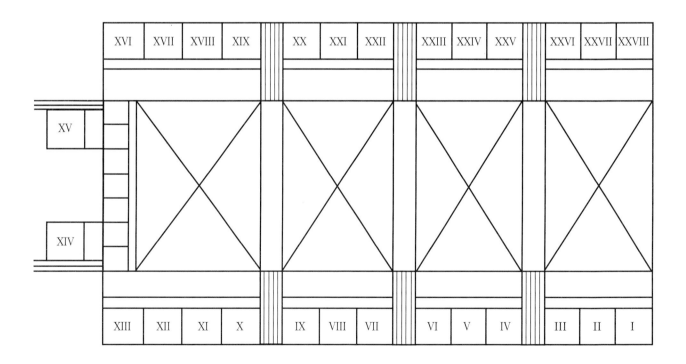

make use of out-and-out *coups de théâtre*. One day he got the people of Assisi to gather in the square and, when he had finished preaching, told them not to go away. Then he went into the church of San Rufino and, taking off his habit, "ordered Brother Pietro to drag him naked in front of the people, with the cord he had round his neck. He commanded another friar to take a bowl filled with ash, climb onto the platform from which he had been preaching, and from there to throw and pour it onto his head."

In the years during which the *Legend of Francis* was being painted, the *Meditations on the Life of Christ* were extremely popular. In this book, the narrator continually urged the reader to "look at" and "see" the events in the Holy Scriptures and to "sympathize" with the passion of Our Lord. In the same way St Francis's exhortation to penitence was lent force by the contemporary character of the saint's life, which was not set in the mists of the remote past and the exotic locations of medieval hagiography, but unfolded in the streets of Assisi and in the Umbrian landscape, amidst familiar faces and everyday problems. The true innovation of the *Legend of Francis* lies in its faithful representation of the theater of life. In the absence of canonical precedents, there could be no iconographic conventions. The scenes are conceived as parts of a landscape that goes on beyond the breaks caused by the spiral columns, a drama performed by actors on improvised stages set up in the city's squares, with theatrically exaggerated gestures and emotionally charged poses. The narrative cycle is presented as the official illustration of the saint's life and miracles, at the behest of the moderate section of the Order and with the approval of the Roman Curia, to facilitate the communication of Francis's message to the throngs of pilgrims.

Following the scheme of a sermon, the life of the saint is divided into groups of three scenes by the painted architecture, each scene forming the theme for mediation in the space of each bay. The scenes on the north wall exemplify the analogy of Francis with the Patriarchs. The first triplet begins with *Francis honored by a Simple Man* (I), followed by *The Gift of his Mantle to a Poor Knight* (II), and ends with *The Vision of the Palace filled with Weapons* (III): the presage of the young man's future exploits passes through the compassionate renunciation of earthly glories and takes concrete form in the promise of divine reward. The patriarch is Noah, saved from the Flood by his faith in God.

The second triplet commences with *The Prayer in front of the Cross in San Damiano* (IV), continues with *The Renunciation of his Father's Inheritance* (V), and concludes with *The Dream of Innocent III* (VI): Christ's invitation to repair the crumbling building passes through the sacrifice of worldly ties and takes concrete form in the recognition of the saint's mission to support the Church.

The patriarch is Abraham, who made a pact of alliance with God.

The third triplet starts with *The Confirmation of the Rule* (VII), goes on with *The Vision of Francis borne on a Fiery Chariot* (VIII) and ends with *The Vision of the Throne reserved for Francis in Heaven* (IX): the blessing given by Innocent III to his beloved Francis makes the saint into a new Elijah come to redeem the world and prefigure its heavenly glory. The patriarch is Jacob, who obtained the birthright from his father Isaac.

The rhythm changes in the wider entrance bay, which is divided into four episodes. The first of these is *The Expulsion of the Devils from the City of Arezzo* (X), followed by *The Ordeal by Fire before the Sultan of Egypt* (XI) and *St Francis in Ecstasy* (XII), while the last is *The Crib at Greccio* (XIII): Francis's humility restores peace to Arezzo and prompts him to preach peace among the unbelievers; his strength lies in his faith in Christ Crucified whom he saw embodied in the festival of Christmas. The patriarch is Joseph, who restored peace among his brothers through his love of justice.

Two episodes are located on the wall at the sides of the entrance, *The Miracle of the Water that gushed from the Rock* (XIV) and *The Preaching to the Birds* (XV): burning with the love of Christ, Francis holds sway over inanimate things and living creatures. The explanation is provided by the two scenes from the New Testament above, the *Descent of the Holy Spirit* and the *Ascension of Christ into Heaven*, which are intended to represent Christ charging the apostles to continue his mission on earth.

On the southern wall the frescoes are read from east to west. The story of Francis is compared with that of Christ depicted on the upper part of the wall and proceeds backward to the reunification with the Heavenly Father; it does not follow the straight line of his earthly biography but the divine scheme of history. The bay next to the entrance is divided into four episodes. The first is *The Death of the Knight of Celano* (XVI), followed by *St Francis Preaching before Honorius III* (XVII) and *St Francis Appears to the Chapter in Arles* (XVIII), and the last is *St Francis Receiving the Stigmata* (XIX): Francis spiritually passes on his prophetic spirit and the power of his preaching to his brothers, and identifies totally with Christ on Mount La Verna.

The tripartite scheme is resumed in the third bay. It starts with *The Death and Funeral of Francis* (XX), continues with *The Vision of Brother Augustine and the Bishop of Assisi* (XXI), and terminates with *The Verification of the Stigmata* (XXII); Francis's similarity to the humble and crucified Christ, revealed in a vision at the moment of his passing away, is confirmed by the discovery of the stigmata on his dead body.

The second bay commences with *Clare taking Leave of*

the Saint's Remains in San Damiano (XXIII), followed by *The Canonization of St Francis* (XXIV), and ends with *The Appearance to Gregory IX* (XXV); the fame of Francis's sanctity, publicly revealed on his death, receives official recognition from the Church and is proved by miracles. The first bay is devoted entirely to miracles worked by the saint, *The Healing of a Devotee of the Saint* (XXVI), *The Confession of a Woman Raised from the Dead* (XXVII), and *The Liberation of the Repentant Heretic* (XXVIII); Francis's conformity to Christ raises him above ordinary miracle-working saints and leads to him being invoked as savior.

Such a dense program required close collaboration between the painter and the friars whose task it was to make sure that the pictures were faithful to Bonaventura's text, slowing down the pace of its execution. Two hundred and seventy-two *giornate*, i.e. portions of painted plaster, each representing one day's work, have been counted in the cycle, but recent investigations suggest that the number was actually higher than this. At times the painter was obliged to modify scenes that had already been finished. In the first version of the *Confirmation of the Rule* (VII) St Francis was depicted standing up; at this point the *giornata* was redone and the saint placed on his knees at the foot of the papal throne. Bearing in mind that it would have been difficult for the painter to work in fresco during the winter, no less than two solar years must have been required to complete such a vast undertaking. A *terminus post quem* is provided by the *Dream of Innocent III* (VI), in which what is left of the ruined Lateran is preceded by a portico adorned with mosaics that Nicholas IV had built in 1291. A *terminus ante quem* comes from *Francis honored by a Simple Man* (I), where the tower of the Palazzo del Capitano appears as it was before its completion in 1305. Outside Assisi, the decorative cycle of the *Legend of Francis* was already known to the fresco painters of the Sala dei Notari in the Palazzo dei Priori in Perugia, finished in 1299. The date can be pinned down even further by the observation that the three popes who appear in scenes VII, XVII, and XXV – Innocent III, Honorius III, and Gregory IX – have the same cast of features, which has been seen as a lifelike portrait of Boniface VIII, elected in December 1294 and a man who placed considerable importance on self-promotion. Ascending the papal throne after it had been renounced by Pietro Celestino, Benedetto Caetani had portraits of himself put on display in Anagni, Orvieto, Bologna, Rome, and Florence; these statues were the motivation for the grotesque proceedings for idolatry that were brought against him after his death by Philip the Fair of France. In January 1296 Boniface VIII granted a solemn indulgence to the tomb of the saint that would hold good every year on the saint's feast day and the seven following days, to encourage the influx of pilgrims and bolster the collection of offerings.

The oldest reference to the presence of Giotto in Assisi is in the *Compilatio Chronologica* by Riccobaldo Ferrarese (1312-13), which praises his work for the Franciscan churches of Assisi, Rimini, and Padua, as well as in the Town Hall and Arena Chapel in the latter city. But the first author to mention the name of the Florentine painter in connection with the *Legend of Francis* was Giorgio Vasari, in the second edition of his *Lives* (1568): "After this [his work in Arezzo] Giotto went on to Assisi in Umbria, having been summoned there by Fra Giovanni di Murro della Marca, who at that time was minister-general of the Franciscans; and at Assisi in the Upper Church of San Francesco, on the two sides of the church under the gallery that crosses the windows, he painted thirty-two histories from the life and works of St Francis. There are sixteen frescoes on each wall, and they were so perfect that they brought Giotto tremendous fame."

The attribution of the cycle to Giotto is not unanimously accepted by students of medieval painting and has met and still meets with strong opposition, especially in English-speaking countries, but it has received unexpected support from the very recent discovery in a private collection of a large *Maestà* with a cryptographic signature by Giotto, which has been identified as the panel by Giotto that Lorenzo Ghiberti remembered having seen in the Roman church of Santa Maria sopra Minerva. Research carried out by Filippo Todini has confirmed that the picture was painted for the Dominican Guillaume Durand, bishop of Mende, who died in Rome on November 1, 1296, and was buried in a tomb that can still be seen in the aforementioned church. The Madonna was painted by Giotto in accordance with the stipulations of his will, as is demonstrated by the date 1297 concealed among the embroideries of the mantle. The style of the Roman painting appears to coincide with a particular stage in the execution of the frescoes in Assisi, that of the first scenes on the south wall, beginning with the *Death of the Knight of Celano* (XVI), which display a clear preference for naturalistic and Gothic effects. So if Giotto was in Rome in 1297, it may be concluded that by this date his contribution to the *Legend of Francis* was over or nearly so.

A similar parallel in the work of the great Tuscan painter can be found in the celebrated altarpiece depicting *The Stigmata of St Francis* in the Musée du Louvre, originally from San Francesco in Pisa and signed "OPUS JOCTI FLORENTINI." The main scene – which is the oldest example of a narrative altarpiece in medieval painting – and the three small scenes on the predella (*Dream of Innocent III, Confirmation of the Rule,* and *Preaching to the Birds*) are faithful reproductions of the frescoes in Assisi. The altarpiece in the Louvre is of great importance for the insight it offers into Giotto's

artistic development prior to his work for the Scrovegni, revealing a preference for a subtle linear cadence and for precious effects that recall the contemporary sculpture of Giovanni Pisano: a Gothic touch that is absent in earlier paintings, such as the *Madonna* in the Parish Church of Borgo San Lorenzo or the *Maestà* in San Giorgio alla Costa in Florence, which are in the manner typical of the scenes of Isaac, still under the influence of the sculptures of Arnolfo di Cambio.

The homogeneity of the program of the *Legend of Francis*

does not prevent us from discerning a process of formal development on the walls of the church, most obvious in the different treatment of the painted architecture: this moves from the "mansions" of the earliest scenes, still thirteenth-century in conception but already an advance on the spatial boxes used in the scenes of Isaac, to the depiction of magnificent halls in perspective in the central scenes, which return in the Cistercian interior of the *Pentecost,* and concluding in a "band of little tabernacles" in the fantastic inventions of the last episodes, metaphysical in flavor and in this very similar to the miniature theaters of his Paduan paintings. Then in the depiction of the human figure we see a gradual abandonment of the more old-fashioned technique of leaving the *verdaccio* primer visible to obtain effects of chiaroscuro, and its replacement by a more luminous palette and the use of cross-hatching to produce the effect of modeling, with the light and shade represented by the paint itself. In his *Libro dell'Arte,* Cennino Cennini describes this technique as typical of the great Tuscan master.

About halfway along the southern wall, from the *Funeral of the Saint* (XX) onward, the compositions grow more crowded, something that can only partly be ascribed to the requirements of the episodes themselves, and a crude realism begins to emerge in the representation of emotions, along with the use of more stylized and elongated forms. This has been imputed to extensive intervention on the part of members of the workshop, and of local painters in particular. The work of the main collaborator in Assisi can be seen in the frescoes of the south transept of Santa Chiara, which are ascribed to an "expressionistic Master of Santa Chiara." There are sound reasons for thinking that this painter was a certain Palmerino from Siena, whose presence in Assisi before May 1299 is recorded by a document attesting to his ownership of a house not far from the church of San Francesco.

Giotto, Francis honored by a Simple Man *(I). The fresco opens the cycle with a homage to the saint's native city, represented here by the civic magistracies and the notable buildings of Assisi; the portico of the Roman temple of Minerva, the Torre del* Popolo, and the Palazzo del Capitano with the coats of arms of Assisi. In reality, it was the last to be painted, as is indicated by the style, common to the scenes that close the cycle.*

Giotto, Francis giving his Mantle to a Poor Knight *(II);* The Vision of the Palace filled with Weapons *(III). The two frescoes were the first part of the decoration of the upper nave to be executed. Unlike in the frescos on the upper wall, the responsibility was entrusted to Giotto alone, who worked on them with the help of numerous assistants. The decision* entailed a prolongation of the time required for execution and the emergence of notable differences between the scenes. We do not know whether this is due to the involvement of different artists or to the evolution that Giotto's figurative style underwent over this period.

Giotto, The Prayer in front of the Cross in San Damiano *(IV);* Francis's Renunciation of his Father's Inheritance *(V);* The Dream of Innocent III *(VI). These frescoes make up the second triplet of the Legend. The last two episodes had already been represented by the "St Francis Master" in the lower church. In* the image of the conversation with the Crucifix Giotto *deliberately exaggerates the ruinous state of the church, later restored by St Francis, and copies the antiquated iconography of Christ from the* Crucifix of the Miracle, *venerated as a relic in the nun's choir of Santa Chiara.*

Giotto, The Confirmation of the Rule *(VII);* The Vision of Francis borne on a Fiery Chariot *(VIII);* The Vision of the Throne reserved for Francis in Heaven *(IX). In spite of the large number of ecstatic states and visions, of which two of the* most miraculous are reproduced on this page, the frescoes in the cycle present St Francis realistically and historically, accompanied by easily recognizable figures of his time.

Giotto, The Expulsion of the Devils from the City of Arezzo *(X);* The Ordeal by Fire before the Sultan of Egypt *(XI);* Saint Francis in Ecstasy *(XII);* The Crib at Greccio *(XIII). These are the four episodes that make up the end of the nave wall. The most famous of them depicts the Tuscan city enclosed by a high wall and represented by brightly-colored houses. The Gothic church behind the saint is the monumental old cathedral of Arezzo, which was located outside the city walls in Giotto's time.*

80

Giotto, The Miracle of the Water that gushed from the Rock *(XIV);* The Preaching to the Birds *(XV). These are the scenes on the inside wall of the facade and among the most celebrated in the cycle. The first is set in a mountainous landscape where rocks are arranged behind the figures, amplifying their gestures. This imparts a symbolic dimension to nature, a* foretaste of the magical realism of the Scrovegni Chapel. In the second, Francis speaks to the birds against a luminous landscape. The scene is constructed around an empty space, devoid of references to the landscape or architecture, traversed by the flight of birds and with the line of the horizon set only just above the feet of the two friars.

Giotto, The Death of the Knight of Celano *(XVI);* Saint Francis preaching before Honorius III *(XVII). The first scene is the one that visitors encounter as they enter the church, on the left wall. The episode was chosen to encourage pilgrims to take the sacrament of confession, following the teachings of St Francis.*

The scene on the right is actually a homage to Boniface VIII, who granted a solemn indulgence to the church of Assisi in January 1296. The pope's appearance is known to us from numerous sculptures.

Giotto, Saint Francis appears to the Chapter in Arles *(XVIII);* Saint Francis receiving the Stigmata *(XIX). In the first scene, set inside a vast chapterhouse opening onto a cloister, Giotto achieves one of his best results in the representation of spatial depth. For the second episode, very close from an iconographic* point of view to the panel in the Louvre *(page 66), the painter drew on St Bonaventura's account of the "Legenda major," where it is stated that Christ crucified appeared to the saint in the semblance of a seraph.*

Giotto, The Death and Funeral of Francis *(XX);* The Vision of Brother Augustine and the Bishop of Assisi *(XXI);* The Verification of the Stigmata *(XXII). An entire bay is devoted to the death of St Francis. The scenes reveal the emergence of a style of painting, characterized by the large number of figures* involved in the events and an increasingly extensive participation by assistants with their personal manners. Nevertheless the elegance of the figures and the Gothic forms of the architecture do have a parallel in certain works by Giotto.

Giotto, Clare taking Leave of the Saint's Remains in San Damiano *(XXIII);* The Canonization of Saint Francis *(XXIV);* The Appearance to Gregory IX *(XXV). With the halt made by the coffin of St Francis at San Damiano for a last farewell to St Clare, the ceremony of canonization in the presence of Gregory IX, and the dream of Gregory IX, ample space is given to the official recognition of Francis's sanctity and to the promotion of the cult of the stigmata on the part of the Church of Rome.*

Giotto, The Healing of a Devotee of the Saint *(XXVI);* The Confession of a Woman raised from the Dead *(XXVII);* The Liberation of the Repentant Heretic *(XXVIII). The Legend of* Francis *closes with three miraculous episodes. The choice of the miracles is indicative of the new concept of sanctity promoted* by the Church at the end of the thirteenth century, which *placed the emphasis on his orthodox attitude toward the sacraments and the efforts he made to save souls rather than on the wonder-working powers celebrated in the early portraits of St Francis.*

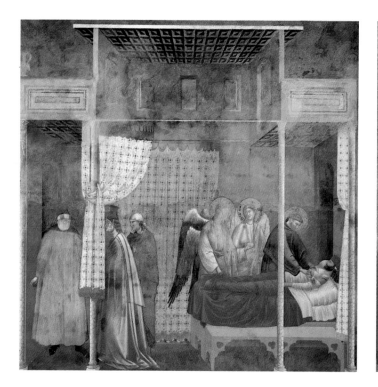

The Construction of the Chapels
in the Lower Church

The scaffolding used by the painters in the upper church had only just been dismantled when the vaults underneath began to ring with the hammers and trowels of masons. It has already been pointed out that the lower church had been built with a single nave divided into bays roofed with cross vaults, with a barrel-vaulted transept and an entrance atrium. The presbytery, where the saint's body was housed underneath the altar, was separated from the area of the lay congregation by an accessible rood-screen, provided with an altar where the mass for the people was celebrated. The church was illuminated by narrow single-light windows in the middle of each bay, in the apse, and in the walls of the transept. This situation was radically modified in the years spanning the thirteenth and fourteenth century, when a new double portal opening onto the lower square was built; the rood-screen at the end of the nave was demolished; holes were knocked in the ends of the transept to build two chapels for the nobility; the two single-light windows in the eastern wall of the transept were blocked up; more holes were knocked in the northern walls of the nave to provide access to three chapels, connected by passages running behind the cylindrical buttresses of the north transept and atrium; large symmetrical arches were opened in the southern wall, but the existence of the sacristy and bell tower meant that these chapels were given a different plan; and a chapel was built at the end of the atrium opposite the entrance. All these works entailed the destruction of any stained-glass that may have been in

the windows of this interior and did irreparable damage to the fresco decoration of the walls, making its correct interpretation impossible.

The reasons for these profound alterations have to be sought in ideas antithetical to the one that inspired the iconographic program of the upper church, founded on an exclusive alliance between the Roman papacy and the Order of the Friars Minor. The new forms of religious life among lay people that emerged at the end of the Middle Ages and the demand for private sepulchers alongside the tombs of the new saints persuaded the friars at the Chapter held in Paris in 1292 to relax the earlier ban on burial in their churches. In doing so they had to overcome the resistance of the secular clergy, who feared a substantial loss of income from legacies. The consequences of this decision soon became apparent in newly constructed buildings, such as Santa Croce in Florence where the entire perimeter of the presbytery was lined with the chapels of noble families.

Another new factor was the concession of the plenary indulgence known as the *Perdono della Porziuncola*, which persuaded ever growing numbers of people to make the pilgrimage to visit the tomb of the new apostle in Assisi. The construction of a small service aisle was intended to permit pilgrims, on the days when the church was most crowded, to reach the confessio under the high altar and to leave again through the side chapels. It is likely that the three northern chapels were built on the initiative of the friars of the Convent itself, and it was not

Giovanni di Bonino, mosaic on the lower portal. The small figure of St Francis that decorates the portal of the lower church is probably the work of the mosaicist from Assisi, who may have executed it in the second decade of the fourteenth century, before his documented activity in Orvieto Cathedral.

until later that they began to look for patrons to sustain the cost of their decoration and of the masses celebrated in them. The chapel of the Magdalen, adjoining the transept, was acquired by the Bishop of Assisi, Teobaldo Pontano. The Franciscan Cardinal Gentile da Montefiore (d. 1312) was temporarily buried in that of St Louis of Toulouse, adjoining the atrium, until the chapel of St Martin that he had had commissioned could be completed. The intermediate chapel, dedicated to St Anthony of Padua, did not find a purchaser until much later, around the middle of the fourteenth century, when it was acquired by the Lelli family of Assisi who placed their own coat of arms in it. Even the passages between one chapel and the next were used as burial places, to satisfy demands by the laity or the convent. The space between the chapels of the Magdalen and St Anthony of Padua, dedicated to the Blessed Valentino, contains the tomb of Fra Hugo de Hertepol, who died in 1302, and this provides us with a *terminus ante quem* for the conclusion of the works.

The third factor was the enormous growth in religious activity among women with a secular and penitential vocation. Angela da Foligno, Margherita da Cortona, Chiara da Montefalco, and Margherita da Città di Castello left a deep mark on the society of the day, building up a huge following among those women who, while wishing to respond to the call of the Lord, did not want to be shut up inside the walls of a strict cloister. By the second half of the thirteenth century the pious bequests to the basilica of Assisi made by women already outnumbered those by men, and it was probably to allow women access to the tomb that the rood-screen set at the end of the nave was demolished. A confraternity of penitent women used the church for its meetings and in 1343 they were granted the use of a chapel, probably that of St Catherine in the atrium opposite the entrance.

Local stonemasons were involved in the construction of the chapels, and it is to them that we owe the lively sculptural decoration of the capitals and other architectural elements, adorned with motifs of leaves from which peer human faces. The subtle difference between the ornaments can be ascribed to the division of the work among various craftsmen, but they are not so marked as suggest the intervention of sculptors from outside. These same craftsmen from Assisi were also responsible for the monument of the Cerchi (?) family set in the atrium and for the church's beautiful portal, executed in the first two decades of the fourteenth century, which resembles precious lace embellished with gilded glass and mosaics. The *St Francis* in mosaic set in the middle of the doorway, formerly thought to date from the eighth decade of the thirteenth century and to be in the style of the "St Francis Master," is actually inspired by the style of the Giottesque frescoes in the chapels of the lower church and may be an example of the mosaic work of Giovanni di Bonino from Assisi, who is documented as having worked on Orvieto Cathedral in the dual capacity of glass painter and mosaicist.

The Decoration of the Chapel of St Nicholas

The chapels of St Nicholas and St John the Baptist located at the ends of the transept were built by Cardinal Napoleone Orsini at the end of the thirteenth century. The coat of arms of the Orsini family is repeated fifty-nine times on the outside and inside walls of the two chapels, but must have appeared no less than ninety-one times if we count the missing bearings whose marks can still be seen. The name and portrait of the donor appear in both the stained-glass windows and the frescoes. The Orsini coat of arms is also engraved all over the fine wrought-iron screens.

Napoleone Orsini is known to have had close ties with the Minorite Order, and in particular with the fringe of the Spirituals. In 1288 Nicholas IV appointed him Cardinal of Sant'Adriano; in 1294 Celestine V made him the protector of the Poor Hermits, a group of Franciscans from the Marche who had split off from the Order under the leadership of Pietro da Macerata and Angelo Clareno; he was personally acquainted with Chiara "della Croce" da Montefalco, preparing the case for her canonization at the behest of John XXII, and with the mystic Angela da Foligno; from 1306 to 1308 his chaplain was Ubertino da Casale, whom Dante names as the head of the Spirituals.

The circumstances of the construction of the chapel of St Nicholas are related by Jacopo Stefaneschi in his *Opus metricum* devoted to the life of St Peter Celestine. While the cardinals were holding a conclave in Perugia to elect a successor to Nicholas IV (d. 1292) – a conclave that lasted for two years without agreement being reached – news arrived of the death of the young Gian Gaetano Orsini as the result of a commonplace riding accident. Moved by their grief – his brother Napoleone was a member of the college – the cardinals decided to bury their differences and unanimously elected a hermit from

the Abruzzi called Pietro da Morrone, who was consecrated pope on August 29, 1294 under the name of Celestine V. He abdicated the pontificate on the following December 13. Napoleone Orsini then had a chapel built in the church in Assisi and buried the body of his brother Gian Gaetano there, in a tomb set above the altar.

The chapel is polygonal in shape, with a short avantcorps roofed with a barrel vault and a pentagonal interior with a domical vault, onto which open three windows with two lights. The sepulchral monument is set in a niche above the altar, with the recumbant effigy of the dead man placed inside a mortuary chamber and indicated by two angels. The reliefs were carved by an Umbrian sculptor, probably of local origin, who had links with the construction of Orvieto Cathedral. Above the monument is painted a fictive triptych with *The Virgin and Child between St Nicholas and St Francis*, depicted in the act of interceding for the deceased.

The pictorial decoration of the chapel is devoted to St Nicholas of Bari, in homage to the donor's uncle, Nicholas III Orsini, whose secular name had been Gian Gaetano like that of the deceased and who had commissioned a chapel containing his tomb in St Peter's. It comprises the stained-glass windows – representing the young Gian Gaetano Orsini presented to the Redeemer by St Francis in the presence of his brother Napoleone, St Nicholas, and other saints – and twelve scenes from the life and miracles of St Nicholas painted on the ceiling and walls, busts of saints in the splays of the windows, and full-length figures of saints on the underside of the arch leading into the church. A scene of the chapel's dedication is painted above the arch of the entrance on the southern wall: the Redeemer receives the homage of Gian Gaetano Orsini, presented by St Nicholas, and

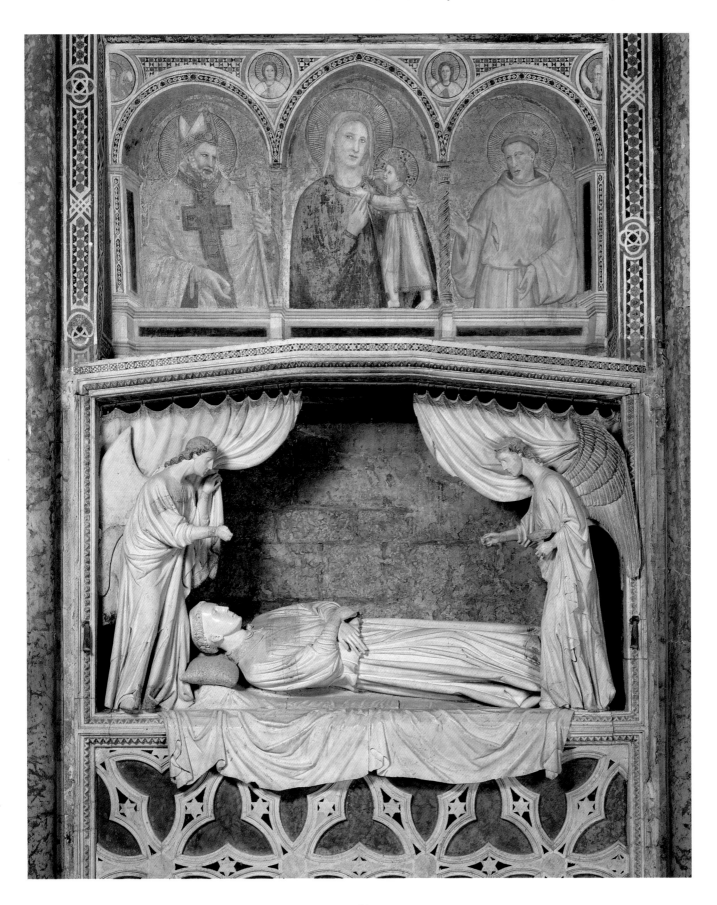

Palmerino di Guido, Saint Nicholas throwing the Gold Bars to Three Poor Girls, *chapel of St Nicholas. The three Scenes from the Life of Saint Nicholas illustrated here, like the others that run along the upper part of the chapel, are all painted in the realistic style of the school of Giotto. Their most likely author is*

Palmerino di Guido, who worked alongside his master on some of the episodes in the Legend of Francis.

Palmerino di Guido, Saint Nicholas forgiving the Consul, *chapel of St Nicholas.*

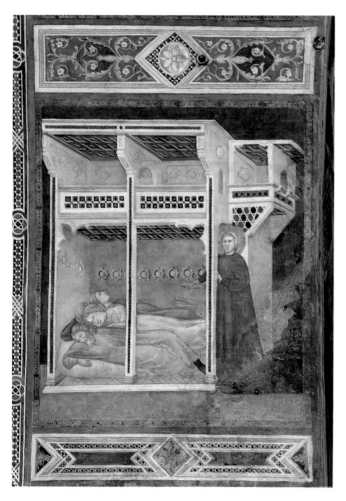

Napoleone Orsini, presented by St Francis. Recent restoration work has revealed that eight kneeling cardinals were originally set alongside Christ; the portraits of the two members of the Orsini family were painted on a new patch of plaster and the figures of the cardinals painted over, for a reason which is not yet clear.

Coming to the authors of the frescoes, the *Scenes from the Life of St Nicholas* reflect the evolution that took place in Giotto's artistic language between the *Legend of Francis* and the Arena Chapel in Padua, and the emergence of a cohesive team of collaborators capable of freely interpreting the directions of the master. Recent studies have put forward the name of Giotto for some upper parts of superior quality, but secondary importance, and for the fictive triptych above the monument, which has been compared with the *Badia Polyptych* in the Uffizi attributed to Giotto by Lorenzo Ghiberti. It is possible that the powerful prelate had turned to Giotto – whom he may have met in Rome around 1300, when Giotto executed

the mosaic of the *Navicella* in the portico of St Peter's for Jacopo Stefaneschi – and that the artist had limited himself to overseeing the undertaking, painting a few busts of saints in the splays of the windows – the first parts to be done – and perhaps the *sinopie* of the scenes from the life of St Nicholas and entrusting the completion of the frescoes to dependable collaborators, selected from among his Umbrian and Tuscan assistants trained in the refined and Gothic style of the last scenes from the life of St Francis. Many of the paintings display the unmistakable manner of Giotto's collaborator on the *Legend of Francis,* who has been identified as Palmerino di Guido. Napoleone Orsini was governor of the duchy of Spoleto in 1300-1, the most likely date for the execution of the frescoes, since the stained-glass windows were made slightly earlier and by a different hand. The work of decoration was certainly complete before June 1306, when a contract was signed in the chapel.

Palmerino di Guido, Saint Nicholas saving Three Innocents
from Decapitation, *chapel of St Nicholas.*

The New Decorative Program of the Lower Church

A few ornamental fragments on the cross vault above the altar and Cimabue's *Maestà* are all that remain of the pictorial decoration of the lower transept prior to the construction of the chapels and the demolition of the roodscreen, that had previously prevented lay men and women from entering the part of the church reserved for the friars. With this obstacle removed, the pilgrim entering the nave through the portal had an unimpeded view of the altar, covered by a baldacchino, along with the apsidal tribune behind and the cross vault painted with a starry sky, in a similar manner to the vaults of the nave frescoed by the "St Francis Master." Once the new decoration had been finished, the visitor was offered a view of the *Glorification of St Francis*, glittering with gold in the dim light of the altar candles.

Although incomplete, the program has an organic unity of its own and sets out to represent the providential role of the order founded by St Francis in the history of salvation, in accordance with a popular spiritual interpretation of the prophecies of Gioacchino da Fiore. Indeed the Calabrian friar Gioacchino da Fiore (1145-1202) had constructed a theological and eschatological vision of the history of the world conceived as the image and reflection of the mystery of the Trinity, going beyond the traditional typological correspondence between the Old and New Testament put forward by St Augustine. For Gioacchino the history of humanity corresponded to a grand theophany that was slowly bringing the mystery of the Unity and Trinity of God to light. Thus he divides the history of the world into three great periods, each coinciding with one of the three Persons of the Trinity: "the first was the age of the Father, who is the Creator of the universe; the second is the age of the Son, who humbled himself to take on our corrupt body; the third will be the age of the Holy Spirit, of which the Apostle says: Wherever is the Spirit of the Lord, there is freedom" (Gioacchino da Fiore, *Liber Concordiae*). The age of the Son is now nearing its end and will soon be succeeded by the age of the Spirit, which will be heralded by the appearance of the angel of the Apocalypse bearing the seal of the living God; then the time of perfect charity will come, when the "Everlasting Gospel" will be preached to all men. This vision was repeatedly condemned by the Church but circulated widely among Franciscans. Even St Bonaventura of Bagnoregio was influenced by the writings of Gioacchino da

Fiore, from whom he drew the Apocalyptic image of Francis symbolized by the figure "of the angel who rises from the east and bears on himself the seal of the Living God" set at the beginning of the *Legenda major*.

The vault above the altar-reliquary is divided by ribs adorned with bands into four cells representing the angelic hierarchy – the angel with the stigmata appears twice – and symbols of the Apocalypse. On the keystone is set the vision of the Messiah: "with a garment down to the foot and girt about the paps with a golden girdle. His head and his hairs were white like wool, as white as snow; and his eyes were as a flame of fire... And he had in his right hand seven stars: and out of his mouth went a sharp two-edged sword: and his countenance was as the sun shineth in his strength" (*Revelation*, I, 13-16). St Francis is depicted in the cell to the west, clothed in light like a new Elijah, taken up into heaven and set on a throne supported by a choir of rejoicing angels; the saint is beardless, in accordance with early Christian models of the Apollonian Christ.

The glorification of the saint is accompanied by allegories of the three monastic vows symbolizing the rule, with the symbol of the virtue celebrated at the center of each cell and contrasting examples of the virtue being practiced and the vice being rejected at the sides. To the south is located the allegory of *Obedience*, set in a loggia where a winged friar places a yoke on a kneeling friar, with an angel leading in a layman and a prelate on the left and a centaur representing pride fleeing on the right; above St Francis is celebrated by two angels. To the north is set the allegory of *Chastity*, represented by a young woman shut up in an ivory tower, while in the foreground a young man receives baptism, a symbol of purity; on the left St Francis welcomes a friar, a Poor Clare, and a layman, representing the three branches of the Order, while on the right Penitence drives away the vices. To the east lies the allegory of *Poverty*, i.e. the mystic marriage of St Francis with Lady Poverty which is celebrated by Christ in the presence of hosts of angels; on the left a young man gives a cloak to a pauper, while on the right a nobleman, a friar, and a prelate are mocking a poor man; above two angels are raising a purple robe and a palace into heaven.

The iconographic program of the cross vault above the altar is continued on the walls of the transept and the

apsidal tribune. The decoration of the apsidal vault, known to us from an accurate description by Fra Ludovico da Pietralunga (ca. 1570), was closely linked to the glorification of St Francis. The upper part of the spherical vault was occupied by a winged Crucifix, beneath which two angels in flight crowned a St Francis with arms spread and his cloak open; regular rows of friars and nuns were ranged at the sides of the saint. The complicated scene, inspired by St Bonaventura's *Itinerarium Mentis in Deum,* was never completed and, although it aroused the admiration of Lorenzo Ghiberti and Giorgio Vasari, who attributed it to Stefano Fiorentino, was

destroyed by Cesare Sermei in 1623 to make room for a *Last Judgment.* All that has survived is a small fragment with a *Woman's Head,* now in the National Art Gallery of Budapest, which is in the style used by the painters of the vaulting cells.

The theme of the evangelical nature of Francis returns on the walls of the transept. The decoration of the northern arm is devoted to the mystery of the Incarnation, as an extension of the allegory of *Chastity,* exemplified by the rebirth of the Christian in baptism. Eight large scenes from the life of the Virgin and from the childhood of Christ are depicted on the vault, separated by bands with

109

busts of Prophets: *The Visitation, The Nativity, The Adoration of the Magi, The Presentation of Jesus in the Temple, The Flight into Egypt, The Massacre of the Innocents, Jesus disputing with the Doctors in the Temple*, and *The Return of Jesus to Nazareth*. The *Annunciation* is painted above the entrance of the chapel of St Nicholas. Below it is the *Miraculous Healing of the Boy in Sessa*, split into two episodes by the arch: on the left is set the death of the boy, crushed by the ruins of the house; on the right his raising by Francis. On the west wall is painted the second miracle St Francis worked on a child, the *Raising of the Boy Who fell from the Balcony*; alongside it is a *St Francis indicating Death Crowned*. The eastern wall is occupied by a *Crucifixion* and by Cimabue's *Maestà*.

The decoration of the southern arm of the transept is devoted to the mystery of the Passion as an extension of the allegory of *Obedience*, evoked by a *Crucifix* frescoed at the end of the loggia depicted in the vaulting cell. Six large scenes from the Passion of Christ are frescoed on the vault, separated by bands with busts of Prophets: *Christ's Entry into Jerusalem, Last Supper, Washing of the Feet, Arrest of Christ in the Garden, Flagellation*, and *Road to Calvary*. The wall to the east is occupied by a grand *Crucifixion*. On the west wall are painted *Judas hanging Himself* and the *Stigmata of St Francis*. The rear wall of the transept is divided vertically into two by the arch of the chapel of St John the Baptist and presents four episodes after Christ's death, arranged in an anti-

110

Giotto, Allegory of Chastity, *detail. The image used by the artists for this allegory – a woman shut up in an ivory tower in the act of receiving the crown and palm of victory – was a recurrent one in Franciscan preaching and drew its*

inspiration from courtly poems on the subject of love, such as the "Tesoretto" of Ser Brunetto Latini.

Pages 112-113: view of the north transept of the lower church.

clockwise sequence: *Christ's Descent into Limbo, Deposition from the Cross, Entombment,* and *Resurrection of Christ.*

The reason for the failure to complete the program on the side of the nave has yet to be explained. On the inner part of the arch are painted ten *tondi* with busts of beatified Franciscans; the missing two were never executed. It is not impossible that, for symmetrical reasons, the intention had been to replace the fragmentary thirteenth-century frescoes of the nave with a typological extension of the allegory of *Poverty.* The question of the *usus pauper* of worldly goods was the cause of heated disputes between the opposing factions of those who supported the original Franciscan rule and the friars of the community, but both sides were able to agree, at the chapter general held in Perugia in 1322, on proclaiming the poverty of Christ and the Apostles. John XXII responded by proclaiming the opinion heretical and restoring to the friars the ownership of their convents, removing the cloak of the Papal See conceded by Nicholas III. Following these developments, to justify the doctrine of Poverty would have been seen as a challenge to the Church and this may have been the reason why the decorative program of the lower church was not completed.

Giotto in the Scenes from Christ's Childhood and the Vaulting Cells

Technical analysis of the painted plaster has shown that the decoration of the transept was carried out in three successive phases, separated by clear breaks. The sequence in which the coats of plaster were laid begins on the vertical wall of the end of the north transept, from the *Annunciation* to the *Miracle of the Boy in Sessa*. These paintings are overlapped by the plaster on the underside of the arch of the adjoining chapel of St Nicholas as well as by that of the barrel vault of the transept, always laid from the top to the bottom and proceeding in the direction of the vaulting cells and the left transept. It can be deduced from this that the plan for redecorating the walls of the transept was contemporary with the decoration of the chapel of St Nicholas, and dated from around 1300, and that Cardinal Napoleone Orsini played some part in it. The painter of the *Annunciation* was also responsible for the upper half of the two scenes of the *Miracle of the Boy in Sessa*, including the four female figures on the far right in the episode of the collapse of the house. These are comparable with the group of women present in the scene of *The Confession of a Woman raised from the Dead* (XXVII) from the *Legend of Francis*. This explains the decision to devote this part of the church to the miracles St Francis worked on children, which associate the saint of Assisi with Nicholas of Bari, the highly popular patron saint of children. At this point work on the decoration was interrupted, to be resumed again at the same point several years later by a painter of very different quality. The two scenes of the *Miracle of the Boy in Sessa* were completed to an existing design or *sinopia* and without altering the form of the frames. The only thing that could help us to unravel this complicated tangle would be an identification of the friar kneeling in prayer between St Francis and St Anthony of Padua in the *Crucifixion* of the north transept. His presence suggests that the decision to decorate the church was one taken largely within the Order itself, with or without the help of wealthy patrons.

On resumption of the work, the scaffolding for the painters was mounted under the vault of the north transept, and then shifted underneath the cross vault and the hemispherical vault of the tribune. Work on the walls of the transept had also been interrupted, at the point where the altars of St Elizabeth and the Madonna stand, and would be continued later by Simone Martini and Pietro Lorenzetti.

The *Scenes from the Childhood of Christ* in the north transept are one of the greatest masterpieces of Italian painting of all time and the celebration of a vision of art founded on the quest for physical beauty rather than spiritual truth, a change in attitude for which contemporaries assigned the credit to the Florentine painter Giotto:
"Giotto had a talent of such excellence that there is nothing created by nature, mother of all things and responsible for the continual turning of the heavens, that he did not depict with pencil and pen and brush that did not seem so similar, indeed the very same, so that it very often happens that the visual sense of men is deceived in the things he has done, believing what was painted to be real." (Giovanni Boccaccio, *Decameron*, sixth day, fifth tale).

These characteristics reach a peak in the *Scenes from the Childhood of Christ*, where the old iconographic schemes are altered for aesthetic reasons, yielding results that can only be compared with the contemporary reliefs on the facade of Orvieto Cathedral. A sensation of earthly beauty emanates from the works of architecture painted in almost perfect perspective, from the sumptuous and gleaming colors, and from the humanity that is the protagonist of these pictures. The splendor of the paint itself is enhanced in the vaulting cells above the altar by the generous use of gold, to give a semblance of immortality to the abstract symbolism of the three vows. The innovative character of the work did not escape the painters of the time, and it is no accident that a substantial number of the rare fourteenth-century drawings that have come down to us are copies of these frescoes in Assisi. Numerous contemporary derivations of them can also be found in painting and illumination. They were used as models for the initial letters of an antiphonary written and decorated by Marino da Perugia in 1321 for San Domenico in Perugia, and this provides a precise *terminus ante quem* for the frescoes.

The new decoration of the lower church was a memorable undertaking for the friars of Assisi given that the first centenary of the saint's death (1326) was drawing near. It is natural that they should have turned to Giotto, who, after his successful debut in the *Legend of Francis*, had become very popular among the Minorites, and in the guise of the Order's official painter had been called on to work in many places on the Italian peninsula, including the monasteries of Pisa, Rimini, and Padua, and subse-

Giotto, The Death of the Boy in Sessa, detail. The beginning of a new "giornata", following a long interruption in the work, can be seen in the detail, just above the group of mourners. However the changeover from one artist to another, one of whom was Giotto himself, has not affected the homogeneity of the composition.

quently in Florence, Naples, and Bologna as well. It goes without saying that over the course of his long life Giotto did not work solely for Franciscan churches, but it was thanks to the patronage of the Friars Minor that he acquired the reputation of the greatest painter in Italy. The chronicler Riccobaldo Ferrarese (1312-3) was aware of this, at a time when the artist was still alive: "Giotto outstanding Florentine painter: how great his art is demonstrated by the works he has done in the Minorite churches of Assisi, Rimini, and Padua, in the City Hall of Padua, and in the Arena chapel in Padua."

Over a century later, in San Francesco at Montefalco (1452), Benozzo Gozzoli accompanied his portraits of the saint's early companions and illustrious Franciscans with those of the poets laureate Dante and Petrarch, and a portrait of Giotto at work on a painting. Just two years earlier Lorenzo Ghiberti noted in his *Commentari* that Giotto "painted almost all the lower part in the church of Ascesi

of the order of Friars Minor," without mentioning the *Legend of Francis*. It is clear that in his time the frescoes in the lower church were considered Giotto's mature masterpiece, a very comprehensible opinion in view of the sculptor's own International Gothic style.

Ghiberti's account has been corroborated by a lucky discovery in the archives that shows Giotto to have been present in the Umbrian city some time prior to the date of January 4, 1309, when Palmerino di Guido – a painter of Sienese origin but settled in Assisi, whose work has already been identified in the *Legend of Francis* and the chapel of St Nicholas – repaid a loan of 50 Cortonese lira to a rich merchant of Assisi that he had contracted along with Giotto di Bondone from Florence, who was not present when the document was drawn up. The fact that this was over a decade after the completion of the *Legend of Francis* suggests that Giotto returned to Assisi after the time he spent in Padua working in the basilica of Sant'An-

Giotto, The Death of the Boy in Sessa *(on the left)*; The Raising of the Boy in Sessa *(on the right)*. *The two scenes, located at the end of the north transept, at the sides of the chapel of St Nicholas, form a single episode. The first depicts the collapse of* *a house and the resulting death of the boy, mourned by his mother and other women in the family. The second shows the miracle of his resurrection by St Francis and is set inside a room.*

tonio and for Enrico Scrovegni (1303-4). It was during this second stay of Giotto's in Umbria – the third in reality if we count his contribution to the chapel of St Nicholas – that he painted the frescoes in the chapel of the Magdalen, where the derivation from the *Scenes from the Life of Christ* in the Arena Chapel is evident, as well as in the north transept and vaulting cells.

Giotto was now at the head of a well organized workshop, no longer made up of occasional collaborators who were required to adapt their own style to Giotto's, but composed exclusively of his own proteges, of Tuscan and Umbrian origin, capable of freely following directions as if they were one with their master. This ensured the same high quality of execution in both the figures and the ornaments. Given the large surface area to be covered and the number of *giornate* – 330 divisions of plaster have been counted in the south transept alone, while no comparable count has been made for the north transept and the crossing – Giotto's stay in the city must have lasted several years, only to be abruptly interrupted. In December 1311

Giotto was recorded in Florence and between 1312 and 1313 he was in Rome, where he painted the polyptych for the high altar of St Peter's to a commission from Jacopo Stefaneschi. This painting, assigned to Giotto in Stefaneschi's obituary list, is the work that comes closest in style to the vaulting cells in Assisi.

Seeking a possible reason for Giotto's abrupt departure from Assisi – the continuation of the program in the south transept by the Sienese artist Pietro Lorenzetti excludes the idea that it was because of any presumed heretical character of the images – I am tempted to blame it on a natural event that took place in Assisi in the summer of 1311 and described in a petition sent to the city council on July 16, 1311, by the custodian of the Convent. The custodian urged the communal authorities to take more to heart the prestige and the dignity of the church, regarded even by outsiders as the city's fount of glory, and to take steps to ensure that the building and its ornaments did not suffer damage. During the violent storms of the preceding days, the runoff of rainwater from the city's streets had

made its way into the church, depositing piles of rubbish there, and if the friars had not promply opened the door that led to the cloister, the water would have submerged the altar of St Francis. Consequently he suggested that the water be diverted outside the city walls rather than letting it flood into the square in front of the church.

Owing to the peculiar shape of the lower church, the only paintings that might have been damaged were the ones being executed around the altar. If the church had been flooded, the damp would have prevented the correct execution of the frescoes and forced the painters to interrupt their work for a long time to let the walls dry out. This is in remarkable agreement with what Giorgio Vasari has to say in his life of Stefano Fiorentino, whom he presumed to have painted the incomplete fresco in the apse: "Stefano began this work with the intention of doing it perfectly and would have succeeded, but he was forced to leave it unfinished and return to Florence to attend to some important business." If this was indeed the case, Giotto must have left for Florence and gone on from there

to Rome, leaving off the frescoing of the walls at more or less the same height.

A much debated problem in the critical literature of recent years is the attempt to identify Giotto's collaborators on the walls of the church. There is widespread agreement over the name of Stefano Fiorentino, mentioned by Ghiberti and Vasari in connection with the lost decoration of the apse: a painter much appreciated by the public of his day for the illusionistic naturalism of his figures, his work is difficult to distinguish from Giotto's. The vaulting cells with the *Glorification of St Francis* and the allegory of *Obedience*, as well as numerous figures in the *Scenes from the Childhood*, have been assigned to an anonymous "Master of the Vaulting Cells" – whose work is characterized by his habit of painting enormous, staring eyes, a symbol of heavenly ecstasy. The parts attributed to this master display the same style as some of the stained-glass windows in the chapels of the lower church, traditionally ascribed to the painter and master glazier from Assisi, Giovanni di Bonino.

Giotto, The Visitation. *This is the first scene on the ceiling of the north transept to have been painted after the resumption of work, which had been interrupted after the* Annunciation. *In comparison with the frescoes he painted in the Arena Chapel in Padua, here Giotto has produced a more sweeping composition with a large number of figures.*

Giotto, The Nativity. *In this scene Giotto makes use of traditional iconographic elements drawn from the apocryphal Gospels – Joseph's black mood, the Child looked after by midwives, the announcement by the angels to the shepherds – but accentuates the narrative character of the story.*

Giotto, The Adoration of the Magi. *This composition proved highly popular with contemporary Umbrian painters, who produced innumerable copies of it. The beauty of the figures and the glowing colors indicate here, as in the rest of the cycle, the emergence of a new aesthetic vision centered on the search for physical beauty.*

Giotto, Presentation of Jesus in the Temple. *The scene is set in the presbytery of a Gothic church supported by pillars, around which the various figures are arranged. It should be noted how the sacred story is adapted to the real requirements of the architecture, resulting in curious situations like the figure of St Joseph half-concealed by a pillar.*

Giotto, The Massacre of the Innocents. *The subject is represented by the artist in terms of crude realism. The group of women on the right have great expressive force as they weep over the corpses of the innocent children just as Mary weeps over the mangled body of her Son.*

Giotto, The Flight into Egypt. *Giotto gives this scene a serene setting: a brightly-lit landscape studded with sparse tufts of vegetation, with a curious little tree bowing to the Virgin as she passes, and the group of sacred figures moving timidly forward shrouded in a magical silence.*

Giotto, Jesus disputing with the Doctors. *In this scene, the amazing representation in perspective of the temple in Jerusalem, which develops some of the ideas already to be seen in the* Legend of Francis, *is an extraordinary anticipation, on the part of a fourteenth-century painter, of the scientific perspective of the Renaissance.*

Giotto, The Return of Jesus to Nazareth. *The painter's attention is concentrated on the splendid view of the towers and domes of the holy city – the Jerusalem of the Messianic promise – which bestows an air of the fabulous on the Holy Family as it departs.*

Giotto, Crucifixion. *This is one of the most beautiful scenes in the cycle. The restrained sorrow of the group on the left, including John and the Marys, contrasts with extreme agitation of the angels fluttering around the cross. On the right, behind* Saints Francis and Anthony, *stands the highly realistic figure of a friar. This may be a portrait of the minister-general of the Franciscan order, the provincial minister, or even the custodian of the Convent.*

Pietro Lorenzetti
in the Scenes of the Passion

The third phase in the decoration involved the whole of the south transept and was carried out by the young Sienese painter Pietro Lorenzetti, who covered the walls with a coat of plaster painted in fresco right down to the level of the floor, without any visible breaks. The lower part of the walls, underneath the scenes of the Passion, was painted with pseudo-marble, including the cylindrical pillars under the crossing. In the north transept the members of Giotto's workshop had only decorated the section of wall above the steps of the stairs with pseudo-marble; the traces of painted marble visible in the arch supporting the staircase and on the left-hand wall of the chapel of St Nicholas date from the time of the "St Francis Master." The south transept has a more complete and unitary appearance than the northern one. There the final result displays a number of evident defects: some parts were not finished (the fresco on the vault of the apse which was replaced by a *Last Judgment* in 1623); others have been left with the rough wall or fragments of the thirteenth-century decoration, or have retained even older images (Cimabue's *Maestà*); yet others date from after Giotto's departure (the altar of St Elizabeth frescoed by Simone Martini, the five companions of St Francis above the altar of the Madonna portrayed by Pietro Lorenzetti) or house still later votive images – the beatified Franciscan painted next to the door leading into the chapel of the Magdalen. The unity of execution in the south transept, on the contrary, goes beyond the requirements of the community's iconographic program – the scenes of the Passion – and includes "private" commissions like the *Madonna dei Tramonti* on the altar of St John the Baptist and even the fresco decoration of the chapel of St John the Baptist.

This premise leads to two conclusions. The first is that the decoration cannot have been completed any later than March 1320. On September 29, 1319, the Ghibelline Muzio di Francesco had seized control of Assisi, setting off a chain reaction that led to the victory of the Ghibellines at Nocera and Spoleto and to the war against Guelph Perugia. To meet the huge expenses of the military campaign, Muzio made Bishop Teobaldo Pontano hand over the papal tithes in the month of October. When these proved insufficient, he broke into the private sacristy of San Francesco on March 11, 1320, and seized the papal treasure, transferred there in 1312, along with precious objects that had been stored there by many prelates of the Curia, though he promised to return them. Angered by this theft, John XXII excommunicated Muzio di Francesco and proclaimed a holy war against Assisi. Besieged by the Perugian army, the city surrendered in March 1322. Its walls were demolished and it was forced to swear obedience to its neighbouring rival. To get the treasure back, John XXII placed Assisi under an interdict: no divine office could be celebrated until the measure was revoked, and since the city was unable to pay back the whole of the debt until 1352, the interdict was maintained until that date, except for brief suspensions. On top of all this, the Friars Minor clashed with the pope over the question of poverty in 1322. During these events, Assisi was certainly not the best place to complete demanding pictorial undertakings; after them it was practically impossible.

Another *terminus ante quem* can be deduced from the commission (April 1320) by Bishop Guido Tarlati to Pietro Lorenzetti for the execution of the large polyptych in the parish church of Arezzo, which is what led Giovan Battista Cavalcaselle to identify the Sienese painter as the author of the frescoes in Assisi, which had been variously

assigned by Giorgio Vasari to Giotto, Puccio Capanna, or Pietro Cavallini.

The second conclusion concerns the role played by Napoleone Orsini in the choice of the painter. The cardinal had had a chapel built for himself in San Francesco that was almost identical to that of St Nicholas, except for the greater care taken over the decoration of the wall and the form of the carved capitals, which indicates a slightly later date. The stained-glass windows, marked with the Orsini coat of arms, are also very different, displaying very strong Byzantine influences that were only to be found, at the beginning of the fourteenth century, in Venetian circles. This fits in with the record of a permit issued to *fioleri* (glass workers) from Murano in 1318 to work on windows for the Friars Minor of Assisi. The fresco decoration of the chapel has been lost, except for the triptych representing the *Madonna and Child between St John and St Francis* set above the altar, in which the two saints allude by hand gestures to the presence of the

prelate, destined to be buried in the niche underneath, repeating the situation that had already been tried out in the chapel of St Nicholas opposite. Following the dramatic events of 1319-22, Napoleone had a new tomb prepared for himself in St Peter's in Rome and stated in his will that he should be buried there alongside his mother, as indeed happened after his death in Avignon in 1342. As a result the tomb in Assisi remained empty. At present it houses the reliquary of the Madonna's veil, donated to the church in Assisi by Tommaso Orsini in 1414.

In reality, the powerful Cardinal Orsini must have had a hand in Muzio's rise to power, having looked favorably on the Ghibelline uprisings in Central Italy from Avignon owing to his ties of friendship with the Bishop of Arezzo, Guido Tarlati, who was the main driving force behind them. During the theft of the papal treasure in March 1320, various objects belonging to Orsini were also taken, which Muzio undertook to return. He did so in 1323, by which time he was a fugitive in Todi, paying the sum of

1000 gold florins to the cardinal's proxy in compensation. Proof of Napoleone Orsini's involvement in the decoration of the south transept should be sought in the fact that the fresco inside the chapel of St John predates the *Scenes of the Passion*, something over which all scholars are in agreement. In this case we have a repetition of the situation already encountered in the opposite transept, where the *Annunciation* painted on the outside of the chapel of St Nicholas is also the first episode of the *Scenes from the Childhood.* As Giotto had left Assisi without even completing the paintings in the crossing, the friars must have turned to Pietro Lorenzetti, then at work on the decoration of the Orsini Chapel, entrusting him with the completion of the work. When did this changing of the guard take place? The archives of the Convent record a series of donations made by private citizens in the years 1316-17, in which there are references to work being carried out inside the church, perhaps relating to the decoration of the transept.

The involvement of Pietro Lorenzetti in the work on the church in Assisi was an event of considerable historical importance, and its significance was increased still further by the simultaneous presence in San Francesco of the other leading figure in the emerging Sienese school of painting, Simone Martini. This was a sign of a new development in figurative art. For centuries it had been a tool in the hands of the Church used for the glory of God and the instruction of the illiterate, and this was still its role in the pictorial sermon of the *Legend of Francis*. Now, however, it had become a form of competition among artists, who tried to outdo each other in their variety of creation. Paraphrasing a famous line by the baroque poet Giovan Battista Marino, we can say of Pietro Lorenzetti too that "The aim of the painter is wonder." Thus Pietro retained the custom of dividing up the vault with broad bands adorned with foliage, out of which peer the heads of putti, but he mixed these up with the heads of cats and grotesque faces. He took his inspiration from the architectural perspectives painted by Giotto in the north transept, but enlivened them by setting small lions and angels on the capitals, as on the facade of Siena Cathedral. Pietro was influenced not only by Giovanni Pisano but also by the *drôleries* of Northern European illuminated manuscripts: above the loggia of the *Flagellation* is set a hunting scene, with one angel holding back a dog, another sounding a horn, and a third trying to hit a fleeing hare, while a monkey on a leash ventures onto the architrave. The third model on which he drew in these frescoes was the precious effect of enamelwork, though much of this has now been lost: Pietro dressed his knights in suits of armor of burnished silver and enlivened them with gilt ornaments; he lavished golden frills on the clothes and the architectural frames. But Pietro's main source of inspiration was the spectacle offered by natural phenomena: he painted the first sky streaked by falling stars and the rise and fall of a crescent moon that marks the hours of Christ's Passion; he painted the first cast shadow by setting a bench against the rear wall that intercepts the light from the door; and he painted the first *trompe-l'oeil*, lining up a still life of ampullae on top of a projection. Finally, Pietro depicted the human face in all the variety of its expressions, from laughter and tears to the grimace and scream, evoking the agonizing and passionate atmosphere of the dramatic Lauds staged by the Umbrian disciplinants; the joust of knights beneath Christ's cross seems to refer to the contents of a fourteenth-century laud of the Passion, from the community of Santo Stefano in Assisi.

The image of the *Madonna and Child between St Francis and St John the Evangelist* set above the altar dedicated to the apostle, and with the donor – a layman whose identity is unknown – portrayed in prayer on the fictive predella, represents a separate problem. The painting is known as the *Madonna dei Tramonti*, the "Madonna of the Sunsets," because of the sunlight that falls on it at the close of the day. As a companion to this picture, Simone Martini painted his Madonna above the altar of St Elizabeth in the north transept against a gilded and punched plate of metal, flooding the church with luminous reflections at dusk, in praise of the name of Mary *maris Stella.*

Pietro Lorenzetti, The Entry of Christ into Jerusalem, *details.*

Page 136, above: Pietro Lorenzetti, Last Supper. *The composition reveals the Gothic roots of the artist's figurative style. The precious architecture enlivened with drôleries, the glimpses of a starry sky, and the fantastic domestic interior demonstrate his familiarity with Parisian illuminated manuscripts and the goldsmith's art.*

Page 136, below: Pietro Lorenzetti, The Arrest of Christ. *A scene of great drama and theatrical disposition, with the crowd rushing in from the rocks on the left and apostles fleeing on the opposite side. The moon disappearing behind the rocks is a moving touch.*

Pietro Lorenzetti, The Flagellation before Pilate. *The scene is set inside a deep portico, lined with precious marble and adorned with lively, figured architectural elements.*

Pietro Lorenzetti, The Road to Calvary. *It has the tragic cadence of a procession of Flagellants, like the ones that used to travel along the roads of Umbria on Good Friday, accompanied by the singing of lauds and marching to the rhythm of their scourges.*

Page 140: Pietro Lorenzetti, The Road to Calvary, *detail.*

Pietro Lorenzetti, Crucifixion. *The painter had a very large area available for this scene, over twice the size of the one utilized* *for the analogous scene in the opposite transept. He made use of it to set the crosses of the two thieves alongside that of Christ and to depict a great tournament of knights in festive array.*

Pietro Lorenzetti, Crucifixion, *details. Here we see some of the most beautiful faces painted by the Sienese artist. Contemporary Umbrian painters drew extensively on this rich gallery of portraits.*

Pietro Lorenzetti, The Descent into Limbo. *This is the first of the scenes devoted to the events following the death of Christ. Though it is less inventive than the earlier frescoes, the meeting between the hands of Christ and Adam is handled with great elegance.*

Pietro Lorenzetti, The Deposition of Christ from the Cross. *This is the most tragic scene in the entire cycle of the Passion. The sacred drama, in which all the figures participate with a high degree of emotional intensity, is set in front of a bare backdrop, dominated by the great wooden cross.*

Pietro Lorenzetti, The Resurrection. *A highly effective composition in which the painter succeeds in making the most of the small space available to him by giving the scene an asymmetrical layout. The sleeping guards, depicted with very daring foreshortening, were to constitute a precedent of great significance up to the time of Piero della Francesca.*

Pietro Lorenzetti, The Deposition of Christ in the Tomb. *Lorenzetti must have taken his inspiration for this scene from Duccio di Buoninsegna's* Maestà *in Siena Cathedral. However he attenuates the hieratic dimension of remote Byzantine origin and accentuates the agony of the mourners.*

Pietro Lorenzetti, The Stigmata of Saint Francis. *Located on the stairs leading to the cloister, the scene was intended to remind the friars entering the choir of Francis's passion over the death of Christ.*

Page 147: Pietro Lorenzetti, Madonna and Child between Saint Francis and Saint John the Evangelist *(above); fictive architecture (below). The sacred composition was painted for an altar dedicated to St John. Two donors were depicted in the mock predella but the one on the left, probably a portrait of a woman, has been lost.*

147

Giotto in the Chapel of the Magdalen

Some of the chapels constructed at the end of the thirteenth century were dedicated to patron saints who had been venerated at older altars in the church. This is the case with St Stanislas, the Archbishop of Cracow, who was canonized in Assisi by Innocent IV in September 1253 and immediately afterward had an altar dedicated to him, corresponding to what is now the singing gallery.

It is worth mentioning the stained-glass windows, for these were all that was visible inside the chapels when their gates were closed. The presence of coats of arms in the windows made it possible to identify the owner of the chapel. This is the case with the two Orsini Chapels in the transept and in the chapel of St Louis, marked by the arms of Gentile da Montefiore. The stained-glass windows of the chapel of St Martin have no coats of arms, but bear the portrait of Cardinal Gentile. The windows in the chapels of St Mary Magdalene, St Anthony, and St Catherine may have been installed by the Franciscan community and paid for by the offerings of the faithful. A further line of research is suggested by the exclusive presence of female figures in the windows of the chapels of the Magdalen and St Catherine, as well as by the fact that they were already in existence before the nearby fresco decoration was painted. The chapel of the Magdalen was acquired by the Minorite Teobaldo Pontano, who was Bishop of Assisi from 1296 until his death in 1329. A letter written by Pope John XXII in July 1332 informs us that Teobaldo had spent the sum of six hundred gold florins for the chapel and had supplied the vestments necessary for performing the mass. The owner's device – a bridge with three arches – is painted several times on the walls and his portrait appears twice: in bishop's robes at the feet of Assisi's patron saint, Rufinus, and in a Franciscan habit at the feet of Mary Magdalene.

The chapel has a square plan, is roofed with a cross vault, and is illuminated by a large window that takes up almost the whole of the back wall. Two passages link it to the chapel of St Anthony of Padua and the transept. The bishop's body is buried under the floor. The lower part of the wall is lined with large stone slabs with mosaic decorations taken from the rood-screen that used to stand in the nave. The pictorial decoration consists of seven scenes from the life of Mary Magdalene. This is the

oldest cycle of frescoes devoted to the saint to be based on Jacobus de Voragine's *Golden Legend*, in which the three women mentioned in the Gospels – the sinner who anoints Christ's feet, Mary Magdalene freed from the seven devils, and Mary the sister of Martha and Lazarus – are united in the one figure.

The surface of the side walls is divided into two levels by flat moldings with simple geometric ornaments. Contrary to custom, the story does not run from top to bottom but begins with the lower row on the west wall, continues on the same level on the opposite wall, and ends with the three lunettes. West wall: *Christ and the Magdalen in the Pharisee's House, The Raising of Lazarus*; in the lunette, *The Magdalen receiving Holy Communion from St Maximinus*. East wall: *Noli me tangere, The Magdalen's Voyage to Marseilles*; in the lunette, *Ecstasy of Mary Magdalene*. Lunette above the entrance: *The Hermit Zosimus giving a Cloak to the Magdalen*. The failure to follow a chronological sequence was a deliberate choice on the part of the artist, intended to lend greater verisimilitude to the last scenes and to avoid the impression that the Magdalen, raised into heaven, was being pushed through the floor of the scenes above. On the lower part of the walls, at the sides of the passages, there are two panels framed by spiral columns: *St Rufinus with the Donor* and a penitent female saint to the west; *Mary Magdalene with the Donor* and the bust of a female saint. Other female saints are painted on the rear wall at the sides of the window and in the splays. There are four tondi with busts of *Christ, Mary Magdalene, Lazarus*, and *Martha* on the ceiling. Under the entrance arch are set twelve large figures, arranged in pairs on three levels.

These frescoes are unanimously attributed to Giotto and are the work that is closest in date and style to his paintings in the Arena Chapel (1303-4). *The Raising of Lazarus* and *Noli me tangere* are actually reproductions of two of the compositions in Padua, but whereas the latter are compressed by the quadrangular format of the framing, the ones in Assisi spread out horizontally to create a more congenial relationship with the natural space. The color is brighter and more luminous and volumes are represented without chiaroscuro but with colored shadows.

Page 148: Giotto, The Magdalen's Voyage to Marseilles, *detail.*

Giotto, The Raising of Lazarus. *Of the scenes that decorate the chapel of the Magdalen, this is the closest to the frescoes in*

Padua, as far as both style and date of execution are concerned. Scholars are unanimous in attributing this cycle to Giotto, while doubts linger over his authorship of the Legend of Francis *and the* Scenes from the Childhood of Christ.

Giotto, Mary Magdalene with the Donor. *The portrait of Teobaldo Pontano, for a long time the bishop of Assisi, appears twice on the walls of the chapel: here dressed in the habit of the Friars Minor at the feet of Mary Magdalene, and in a bishop's cloak and miter at the feet of St Rufinus.*

Simone Martini in the Chapel of St Martin

The two chapels that open onto the first bay of the nave are marked by the insignia of the Franciscan Cardinal Gentile da Montefiore. The latter had been appointed cardinal, under the protection of St Sylvester and St Martin of Tours, by Boniface VIII. In 1307 Clement V sent him as papal legate to Hungary, where the death of Ladislas IV (d. 1290) had sparked off a war of succession between the Magyar nobility and Ladislas's daughter Maria, the wife of Charles II of Anjou, King of Naples, who claimed the throne for her firstborn son Charles Martel. Gentile's mission was a success and through his mediation Charles Robert of Anjou, the son of Charles Martel (d. 1295), was acclaimed King of Hungary in November 1308. In the meantime, Charles II's second son, Louis, had expressed the desire to become a Friar Minor, renouncing the throne of Naples. In 1296 he was appointed Bishop of Toulouse by Boniface VIII and took his vows before the general of the Order, Giovanni da Muro. He died in Provence the following year, while on his way to Rome to renounce his bishop's rank. So the line of succession passed to the third son Robert, who was crowned King of Naples in 1309. Charles II himself took steps to get the process of canonization of his son Louis under way, although the members of the Order's hierarchy were not very enthusiastic owing to the young man's Spiritual sympathies. The process did begin in 1307 but it was not until ten years later

that Louis was proclaimed a saint, following the election of a pope friendly to the Angevins, John XXII. These events were to have profound repercussions on the Minorite Order and the mother church in Assisi.

His mission to Hungary over (September 1311), Gentile da Montefiore was summoned back to Italy by Clement V and charged with transferring the papal treasure to Avignon. In March 1312 he was in Assisi and deposited part of the papal treasure in the sacristy of San Francesco. On March 30 he paid the friars of Assisi six hundred gold florins "for a chapel to be made in San Francesco." Leaving Assisi, he was escorted by Perugian troops as far as Siena and by early June was in Lucca, where he died in October 1312. His body was taken back to Assisi and buried in the chapel of St Louis, since the chapel of St Martin was still under construction. The papal treasure and his personal effects remained in Lucca, where they were stolen by the Ghibelline Uguccione della Faggiola. We do not know whether Gentile da Montefiore had the

chapel of St Louis decorated as well. The frescoes of *Scenes from the Life of St Stephen* on the walls date from 1574, when they were painted by the Mannerist artist Dono Doni for a local fraternity. The Franciscan cardinal – or someone acting on his behalf – certainly commissioned the splendid stained glass in the large window, in which his coat of arms is repeated four times. The iconography of the window is based on an openly philo-Angevin political program: the emblem of the Anjou – the fleur-de-lis – forms the backdrop to various figures. St Louis of Toulouse appears twice in the panes on the left: in the guise of a young layman kneeling at the feet of St Francis giving his blessing, and wearing a bishop's mantle over the Franciscan habit alongside Christ giving his blessing. The panes on the right depict the Virgin Mary next to St Louis IX, King of France and great-uncle of the other St Louis, who was himself canonized in 1297; and Cardinal Gentile kneeling at the feet of St Anthony of Padua. The stained-glass windows were designed by the "Master of the Vaulting Cells," already identified as Giotto's collaborator in the frescoes of the crossing, who may have been the painter and stained-glass worker from Assisi, Giovanni di Bonino.

The decoration of the chapel of St Martin also follows a philo-Angevin line, to such an extent that it has been suggested that Robert of Anjou may have played a part in the fulfillment of the prelate's last wishes. In the Pinacoteca di Capodimonte, Naples, there is a large altarpiece painted by Simone Martini for the Franciscan church of San Lorenzo Maggiore in Naples during the same period in which the frescoes of the chapel of St Martin were being executed. It depicts St Louis of Toulouse crowned by two angels while he in turn crowns his brother Robert, kneeling at his feet. The Angevin lilies and the Hungarian coats of arms that are dotted all over the picture confirm the official purpose of the altarpiece, intended to quash the arguments over St Louis's support for the Spirituals and the regularity of Robert of Anjou's ascent of the throne.

The chapel of St Martin is a rectangular room covered by a barrel vault and ending in a hexagonal apse containing three large two-light windows decorated with splendid stained-glass. The lower part of the walls is faced with inlays of stone from Assisi, in which the donors coats of arms are inserted. Gentile's emblem is repeated several times in the splays of the windows and his portrait

appears twice: kneeling at the feet of the saint as Pope Martin I in the lowest part of the central window and in the scene of dedication on the inside of the front wall, holding out his hand to St Martin dressed as a bishop.

The decoration of the walls is devoted to St Martin of Tours, Cardinal Gentile da Montefiore's patron saint, perhaps selected in part for the devotion shown to him by St Francis and his role as apostle to Gaul, which made him particularly popular with the political patrons of the donor. The walls are divided into two levels, separated by geometric frames with busts of angels at the top. The saint's life is represented in ten episodes, starting from the east wall and running first along the bottom row and then along the top: *St Martin sharing his Cloak with a Beggar at the Gate of Amiens; Christ appears to Him in a Dream carrying the Cloak; He is made a Knight by Emperor Julian; He renounces Arms and faces the Enemy with Nothing but a Cross; He raises a Boy from the Dead in Chartres; The Dream of St Ambrose; Angels cover St Martin's bare Arms, in Gratitude for having given his Tunic to a Pauper; Emperor Valentinian falls to his Knees at the Saint's Feet; the Death of the Saint; his Funeral in the Miraculous Presence of St Ambrose.* The splays of the windows are decorated with busts of saints, divided into lay saints, bishops, and monks. There are eight full-length figures of saints on the underside of the entrance arch:

Francis and *Anthony, Mary Magdalene* and *Catherine, Clare* and *Elizabeth of Hungary, Louis of Toulouse* and *Louis of France*; the latter are painted against a background studded with lilies.

It was not until 1820 that the chapel's frescoes were attributed to Simone Martini by Sebastiano Ranghiaschi, a noblemen from Gubbio who was an amateur restorer and collector of "Primitives." It is likely that the prelate had met the painter during a stopover in Siena on his way to Avignon, at the time when Simone Martini was at work on his celebrated *Maestà* in the city's Palazzo Pubblico, and had commissioned him to decorate the chapel. The *Maestà* was finished in 1315, a date that is visible on the lower part of the frame, but it is probable that it was painted in two separate phases, as is demonstrated by the presence of an obvious break in the plaster about a third of the way up and the difference in style between the upper part and the busts of saints on the frame where the date is inscribed. The oldest parts are still influenced by the example of the founder of the Sienese school of art, Duccio di Buoninsegna. They have been compared with the saints in the stained-glass windows of the chapel in Assisi, and this has led to the hypothesis of an early visit to Assisi by Simone to design the cartoon for the windows – then painted by Giovanni di Bonino – which are customarily held to have been executed before the

Simone Martini, Madonna and Child between Saint Stephen and Saint Ladislas. *The series of saints reproduced in these pages was painted for an altar dedicated to St Elizabeth of Hungary that used to stand in the north transept of the lower church. They are all linked to the Hungarian royal house and the Angevins of Naples, who had strong ties with the Franciscan order and had donated precious pieces of goldwork and church furnishings to the basilica in Assisi.*

frescoes. Giotto's *Scenes from Christ's Childhood* in Assisi made a deep impression on Simone and it is likely that he also went to Orvieto to study the bas-reliefs on the facade of the cathedral. Back in Siena, he painted the busts of saints on the lower frame with a sophisticated naturalism and using techniques that were revolutionary for the time, such as the decoration of their haloes with lozenges. These features also appear in the frescoes in Assisi, which can be dated to some time around 1315.

In Assisi Simone painted images of rare beauty, unsurpassed for a long time to come. His great skill at blending models and materials derived from different techniques allowed him to combine the macrocosm of the clear and measurable spaces of the Giottesque tradition with the microcosm of the minute tooling of the gilded parts in relief, where he made use of the punches carved by goldsmiths for church ornaments. His architectural structures represent the triumph of the northern Gothic cathedral, miniaturized so as to fit into the artificial space of a picture; they are peopled by a deeply characterized set of human figures, on which his perfect mastery of the technique of painting bestows a fragrant breath of life. In his hands the story of the saint's life is imbued with a sense of chivalric pomp and dressed in the fabulous clothes of the Angevin court frequented by Cardinal Gentile. Here Simone reveals himself to be the creator of a modern style that was to become the language current in the aristocratic courts of Europe and that would receive an official consecration when the painter was summoned to Avignon. Art lovers were unable to resist the fascination of his pictures and works were commissioned from him more than once by the aging Napoleone Orsini – formerly the patron of Giotto and Pietro Lorenzetti in Assisi – who had Simone paint his portrait in a picture praised by Francesco Petrarch, as well as the famous small polyptych with scenes from the Passion that is now divided among museums in Paris, Antwerp, and Berlin.

Simone Martini also painted the Angevin saints on the altar of St Elizabeth of Hungary in the north transept. From the left: *St Francis, St Louis of Toulouse, St Elizabeth of Hungary, St Margaret, St Henry of Hungary, St Stephen, Madonna and Child,* and *St Ladislas.* The identity of these figures, all linked to the reigning house of Hungary except the Madonna and St Francis, suggests that the work was an *ex-voto* for the happy conclusion of the intricate problem of the Hungarian succession, offered on the old altar of St Elizabeth. Robert of Anjou and his nephew Charles Robert, Kings of Naples and Hungary respectively, provided the altars of the basilica with precious pieces of goldwork and church furnishings, recorded in the ancient inventories of the sacristy.

Simone Martini, Saint Martin with the Donor kneeling. *This is the large scene of dedication painted on the wall above the entrance. The two figures are portrayed inside a Gothic tabernacle; behind them runs a long balustrade of polychrome marble on which is set the red hat of Gentile da Montefiore, an emblem of his rank of cardinal.*

160

Page 160, above: Simone Martini, Saint Louis, King of France and Saint Louis of Toulouse.

Page 160, below: Simone Martini, Saint Anthony of Padua and Saint Francis.

Simone Martini, Saint Louis, King of France, *detail. Curiously, the figure of the sanctified king was painted at a later date, over a figure dressed in a long white tunic alluding to his office as a priest, still visible in the lower part of the fresco.*

Simone Martini, Saint Martin sharing his Cloak with a Beggar at the Gate of Amiens. *The discovery of the sinopia of the fresco, now in the Treasury of the Convent, has revealed to us the original composition of the scene, which was set between the two opposite gates in the city's ring of walls.*

Simone Martini, The Dream of the Cloak. *Jesus, surrounded by angels and carrying Martin's cloak, appears to him in a dream, revealing that the beggar had been his incarnation. The figure of the sleeping saint is a tour de force on the part of* the artist, with its realistic depiction of the "open" embroidery on the sheet and cushion and of the way the pattern of the blanket is molded to the shape of his body.

Simone Martini, Saint Martin is made a Knight by Emperor Julian. *This is one of the most celebrated scenes in medieval Western painting. It embodies the highest ideals of chivalry: aristocratic etiquette, the virtues of love and courtesy, the* pastimes of hunting and "bel canto", rendered in glowing colors and elegant forms that convey a powerful image of those long-ago times. This fresco does not just represent the Middle Ages, it is the Middle Ages in poetic form.

Simone Martini, Saint Martin is made a Knight by Emperor Julian, *detail.*

Simone Martini, Saint Martin renounces Arms. *The scene is among the tents of a military encampment against a backdrop of bleak hills. The young knight Martin, armed with nothing but a cross, is portrayed taking his leave of the emperor, whose perfect profile has been copied from an antique medal.*

Simone Martini, Saint Martin renounces Arms, *details*.

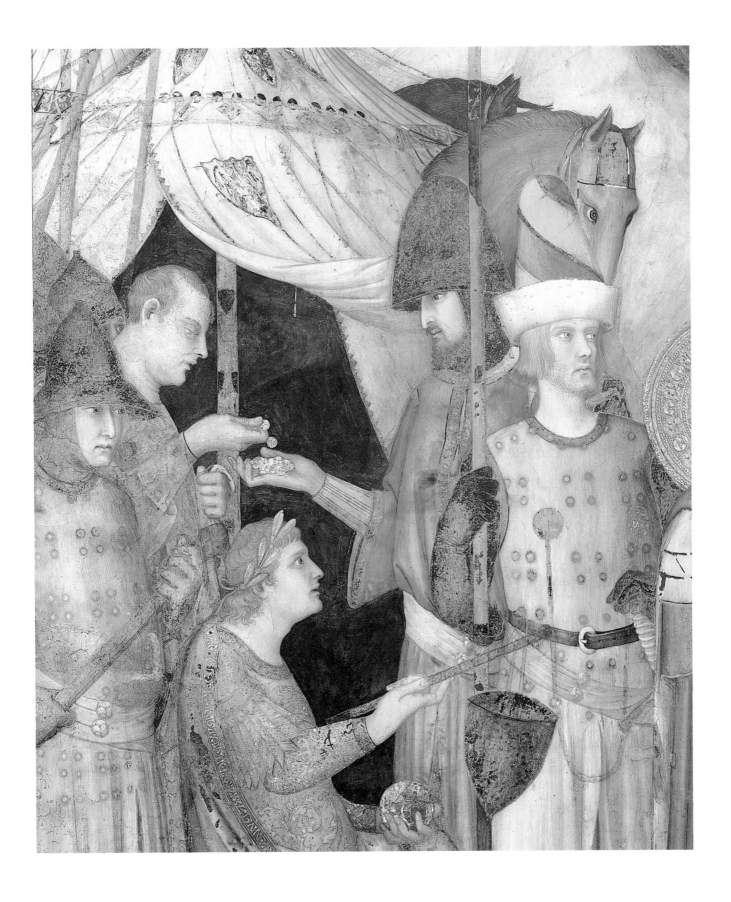

Simone Martini, The Miracle of the Resurrected Boy. *In this scene an old woman dressed as a penitent appears behind the boy's mother. This has been interpreted as a homage to St Clare of Montefalco, an Umbrian mystic who was held in much esteem in the Curial circles of the time.*

Simone Martini, The Funeral of Saint Martin. *The funeral ceremony has the grandeur of a memorable event. The bishop celebrating the office for the dead is St Ambrose, but the identity of the monk with a red cloak is unknown.*

The onlookers constitute an extraordinary gallery of portraits, both for their realistic features and for the painstaking reproduction of their ceremonial costumes. With this cycle Simone Martini attained one of the highest peaks of European art.

Simone Martini, Saint Martin and the Emperor Valentinian. *The emperor is shown kneeling at the saint's feet since, after refusing to see him, he has been hurled to the ground by a tongue of flame springing suddenly from the throne.*

Pag. 183: Simone Martini and Giovanni di Bonino, stained-glass window of the chapel of St Martin.

The Decline of Assisi

The loss of the city's freedom through its submission to Perugia, the continued imposition of the papal interdict as a result of the failure to return the papal treasure stolen by Muzio di Francesco, and the friction between the Church in Avignon and the Franciscan Order over the question of poverty threw Assisi into a state of deep decline in political as well as economic and religious terms. The euphoric state that had been brought about by the construction of the two great mendicant churches of San Francesco and Santa Chiara and the enlargement of the city with a new circle of walls was brought to a sudden halt in the year of 1322.

Religious life was particularly badly affected by the papal excommunication, which was not lifted until 1352, notwithstanding frequent suspensions and the exemption of the church of San Francesco. To avoid its consequences a total of thirteen confraternities were founded, almost all of them Flagellants, which was a disproportionate number for a small community like Assisi: membership of a religious sodality allowed access to the prohibited sacraments and ensured the burial of the dead. A large number of tombs – communal cemeteries of confraternities or graves of individual citizens – were dug in the floor or set against the walls of the Chiostrino dei Morti.

The main consequence for the basilica of San Francesco was the failure to complete the iconographic program of the lower church and the fragmentary state in which the walls of the nave and narthex were left. The only significant work carried out in the church under the interdict was the decoration of the *cantoria* or "singing gallery," set up under a tall blind arch located at the end of the south wall of the nave and enclosed by a balustrade made out of slabs taken from the old rood-screen. At the back of the lunette is set a *Coronation of the Virgin in a Glory of Angels*, whose lower part was left incomplete; two scenes from the life of St Stanislas, the Archbishop of Cracow who had been canonized in Assisi in 1253, are painted under the arch: *St Stanislas raises a Dead Man to testify to his Innocence* and the *Martyrdom of the Saint*; there is a *Crucifixion* above the small altar. The coat of arms repeated in the borders around the scenes is that of the Soldani family from Assisi. The most prominent member of this family was a certain Jolo Soldani who, on his death in 1337, left various bequests to confraternities in Assisi and was buried in the church of

San Pietro. Jolo had a son called Giovanni who became a friar. He was custodian of the Convent for about one year, from 1337 to 1338, and it was probably he who commissioned the decoration.

All this suggests that the singing gallery should be dated to around 1337-8, something which is confirmed by stylistic analysis of the paintings. It is on the basis of these frescoes that the historical figure of Puccio Capanna has been identified. A native of Assisi, he was mentioned by Vasari as one of Giotto's direct pupils, trained by the master in the latter part of his career. Along with the Florentine Maso di Banco, he was Giotto's main heir as well as the leading exponent of that "most gentle and unified" manner that was the greatest innovation in the Italian painting of the second quarter of the fourteenth century, before the upheavals caused by the outbreak of the Black Death in 1348.

Puccio Capanna was also the artist of the large *Crucifixion* in the Chapter House – curiously it too incomplete – where the figures of Louis of Toulouse, Paul, the Virgin Mary, Francis, John, Clare, Peter, and Anthony of Padua are lined up at the feet of a gigantic Christ. It is an extraordinary painting from which emanates a classical sense of proportion and a monumental impetus that foreshadow the work of Piero della Francesca. It is possible that this second fresco, which is generally assigned to the final phase of Puccio Capanna's career before his death from the plague in 1348, was also commissioned by Fra Giovanni di Jolo, who once again held the post of custodian of the Convent in 1344.

The grand period of fourteenth-century decoration was brought to an end with the chapel of St Catherine, which served as a temporary burial place for Egidio Albornoz, the powerful Spanish cardinal sent to Italy by Innocent VI in 1353 to force the cities of the Papal State that had rebelled following the transfer of the papal see to France into submission to the Church. Albornoz financed the restoration of the chapel in 1362, to a design by the architect Matteo Gattaponi from Gubbio, and its pictorial decoration, for which Andrea de' Bartoli from Bologna was paid in 1368. The same year the coffin of the cardinal (d. 1367) was placed in a tomb set behind the altar, where it remained until its transfer to Toledo in Spain in 1372.

The extremely lively pictorial decoration illustrates

Page 184: Puccio Capanna, Coronation of the Virgin, *detail.*

Singing gallery of the lower church. This was carved out of the thickness of the wall, damaging the thirteenth-century pictorial

decoration and reusing the fine slabs of polychrome marble from the old rood-creen. The frescoes in the niche, dedicated to St Stanislas, are a mature masterpiece by Puccio Capanna.

episodes from the life of St Catherine. The stained-glass windows, on the other hand, date from an earlier period, sometime during the second decade of the fourteenth century, and reflect the style typical of Giovanni di Bonino from Assisi, who was also responsible for the windows in the chapels of St Anthony and St Louis. Contrary to what is often claimed, the painted glass is the work of a single artist, with the exception of a few parts dating from later restorations. The need for such restorations is inherent in the fragility of the medium. In 1319 the custodian of the Convent had several copies made of extracts from the Statutes of the Commune of Assisi which prohibited the use of crossbows and slings in the vicinity of the church so as to avoid damage to the windows.

Over the following centuries the mural decoration of the church remained substantially unchanged. Numerous works were carried out inside the Convent during the papacy of the Franciscan Sixtus IV Della Rovere (1471-

Puccio Capanna, The Martyrdom of Saint Stanislas. *The martyrdom of the archbishop of Cracow is set inside a Gothic church, identified by some with the upper basilica of Assisi. The large Crucifix painted for Brother Elias by Giunta Pisano can be seen at the end of the nave.*

84), who commissioned the construction of the two-story arcade in the Renaissance cloister and the oratory of San Bernardino in front of the entrance to the lower church. The Renaissance porch set over this doorway was carved by Francesco di Bartolomeo from Pietrasanta at the time of the minister-general Francesco Sansone (1486-87). The latter also commissioned the great choir stalls of the upper church, adorned with intarsia made in the workshop of Domenico Indivini from San Severino Marche (1491-1501), depicting canonized and beatified Franciscans.

In the years of the Counter-Reformation that followed the conclusion of the Council of Trent (1563), when the change in liturgical requirements forced the modernization of such glorious buildings as Santa Croce in Florence and Santa Maria in Aracoeli in Rome, and when the Sanctuary of Il Perdono was built on the ruins of the first Franciscan holy place of Porziuncola in the Spoleto Val-

ley, a friar from Assisi whose job it was to show visitors round the church, Ludovico da Pietralunga, wrote an accurate description of its "primitive" paintings, pointing out that they represented the roots of Franciscan iconography. In the same years Cardinal Baronio was exploring the passages of the Roman catacombs in search of relics of the early Christian martyrs. This interest in medieval painting was shared by Dono Doni, a local painter who had grown up under the influence of Perugino before starting to imitate the leading exponents of the Roman manner. He too wrote a description of the basilica of Assisi, unfortunately lost, and frescoed the walls of the cloister with *Scenes from the Life of St Francis* (1564-70), basing the iconography of many episodes on the fourteenth-century models. The decoration, which anticipated the work of the reformed Tuscan painters, seems to endorse the claims of the Conventual Minorites to be the

Puccio Capanna, Saint Stanislas raises a Body from the Dead.
The miraculous event is set in the graveyard of a monastery
cloister, while the large church in the background represents
the basilica of St Francis.

Puccio Capanna, Crucifixion, *Chapterhouse. Datable to around 1344, the fresco reveals, in the quality of its color and the classical composure of the forms, the influence of the late Giotto.*

legitimate heirs to the message of St Francis, notwithstanding the fierce criticism to which they had been subjected at the Council and the fears that the branch would be suppressed in favor of the Observant Minorites, from whom they had split in 1517.

Although the seventeenth century was a period in which little respect was generally shown for medieval painting, the modifications made at this time were dictated by the need to restore and maintain paintings that had been subjected to centuries of deterioration, owing to the dampness of their environment, and there can be no doubt that the fragmentary appearance of the frescoes in the lower church and some of the chapels was of concern to more than one member of the Order. The most conspicuous intervention was on the hemispherical vault of the apse, where Cesare Sermei frescoed a *Last Judgment* (1623) as a replacement for the incomplete fourteenth-century decoration. Sermei also decorated the arch in front of the entrance with an image of St Francis showing the text of the solemn indulgences granted to the basilica by Popes Sixtus V and Paul V, and in collaboration with Girolamo Martelli frescoed the walls of the atrium with parallel scenes of the birth of Christ and St Francis (1646-7).

In more recent times, the renewal of interest in the early centuries of Christian art that followed the spread of Romanticism and the emergence of mass tourism with the development of modern means of communication have brought ever growing numbers of visitors to Assisi, modern pilgrims drawn to St Francis's tomb by the undying fascination of the saint and the universal fame of the splendid reliquary that houses his mortal remains, *caput et mater* of Italian art.

On October 27, 1986, the "World Day of Peace" was celebrated in Assisi. Invited by John Paul II, representatives of almost all the religions met in Assisi, for the first time in history, with a single prayer in mind: peace among peoples. Owing to the universal character of Francis's message, Assisi was assigned the privilege and the duty of representing the positive feelings of the different religions about the brotherhood of peoples and respect for the Earth.

ESSENTIAL BIBLIOGRAPHY

Owing to the enormous output of books on St Francis of Assisi, the publications listed here represent no more than a sample of more recent studies. It is suggested that the reader refer to monographic volumes and conference proceedings for further indications.

G. PREVITALI, *Giotto e la sua bottega*, Fratelli Fabbri Editore, Milan 1967.

VAR. AUTHORS, *Giotto e i giotteschi in Assisi*, CEFA, Assisi 1969.

A. MARTINDALE, *The Complete Paintings of Giotto*, London 1969.

P. VENTUROLI, "Giotto," in *Storia dell'Arte*, nos. 1-2, 1969, pp. 142-58.

VAR. AUTHORS, *Giotto e il suo tempo*, conference proceedings (1967), De Luca Editore, Rome 1971.

M. BOSKOVITS, "Nuovi studi su Giotto e Assisi," in *Paragone*, no. 261, 1971, pp. 34-56.

A. SMART, *The Assisi Problem and the Art of Giotto*, Oxford 1971.

M. BOSKOVITS, "Giunta Pisano: una svolta nella pittura italiana del Duecento," in *Arte illustrata*, no. VI, 1973, pp. 339-52.

G. MARCHINI, *Le vetrate dell'Umbria*, De Luca Editore, Rome 1973.

V. MARTINELLI, "Un documento per Giotto ad Assisi," in *Storia dell'Arte*, no. 19, 1973, pp. 193-208.

G. RUF, *Franziscus und Bonaventura*, Assisi 1974.

A. TANTILLO MIGNOSI, "Osservazioni sul transetto della basilica inferiore di Assisi," in *Bollettino d'Arte*, no. LX, 1975, pp. 129-42.

H. BELTING, *Die Oberkirche von San Francesco in Assisi. Ihre Dekoration als Aufgabe und die Genese einer neuen Wandmalerei*, Gebr. Mann Verlag, Berlin 1977.

B. ZANARDI, "Da Stefano Fiorentino a Puccio Capanna," in *Storia dell'Arte*, no. 22, 1978, pp. 115-27.

L. BELLOSI, *Giotto*, Scala, Florence 1979.

F. TODINI, "Una nuova traccia per Giotto ad Assisi," in *Storia dell'Arte*, nos. 38-40, 1980, pp. 125-29.

I. HUECK, "Cimabue und das Bildprogramm der Oberkirche von San Francesco in Assisi," in *Mitteilungen des Kunsthistorischen Institutes in Florenz*, no. XXV, 1981, pp. 279-324.

G. RUF, *Das Grab des hl. Franziskus. Die Fresken der Unterkirche von Assisi*, Verlag Herder, Freiburg i. B. 1981.

VAR. AUTHORS, *Roma anno 1300*. Atti del Convegno, conference proceedings (1980), edited by M.A. Romanini, L'Erma di Bretscheimer, Rome 1982.

FRA LUDOVICO DA PIETRALUNGA, *Descrizione della basilica di S. Francesco e di altri santuari di Assisi*, edited by P. Scarpellini, Edizioni Canova, Treviso 1982.

S. ROMANO, "Le storie parallele di Assisi: il Maestro di S. Francesco," in *Storia dell'Arte*, no. XLIV, 1982, pp. 63-82.

M. BOSKOVITS, "Celebrazioni dell'VIII centenario della nascita di San Francesco. Studi recenti sulla Basilica di Assisi," in *Arte cristiana*, no. LXXI, 1983, pp. 203-14.

J. POESCHKE, "Der 'Franziskusmeister' und die Anfänge der Ausmalung von S. Francesco in Assisi," in *Mitteilungen des Kunsthistorischen Institutes in Florenz*, no. XXVII, 1983, pp. 125-70.

I. HUECK, "Der Lettner der Unterkirche von San Francesco in Assisi," in *Mitteilungen des Kunsthistorischen Institutes in Florenz*, no. XXVIII, 1984, pp. 173-202.

M. ANDALORO, "Ancora una volta sull'Ytalia di Cimabue," in *Arte Medievale*, no. 2, 1985, pp. 84-177.

L. BELLOSI, *La pecora di Giotto*, Einaudi, Turin 1985.

J. POESCHKE, *Die Kirche San Francesco in Assisi und ihre Wandmalereien*, Hirmer Verlag, Munich 1985.

S. ROMANO, "Pittura ad Assisi 1260-1280. Lo stato degli studi," in *Arte Medievale*, no. 2, 1985, pp. 109-40.

I. HUECK, "Die Kapellen der Basilika San Francesco in Assisi: die Auftraggeber und die Franziskaner," in *Patronage and Public in the Trecento*, Olschki Editore, Florence 1986, pp. 81-104.

F. TODINI, "Pittura del Duecento e del Trecento in Umbria e il cantiere di Assisi," in *La pittura in*

Italia. Il Duecento e il Trecento, Electa, Milan 1986, pp. 375-413.

VAR. AUTHORS, *Simone Martini*, conference proceedings (Siena 1985), edited by L. Bellosi, Centro Di, Florence 1988.

M. CHIELLINI, *Cimabue*, Scala, Florence 1988.

C. FRUGONI, *Pietro e Ambrogio Lorenzetti*, Scala, Florence 1988.

S. BRUFANI, *Eresia di un ribelle al tempo di Giovanni XXII: il caso di Muzio di Francesco d'Assisi*, "La Nuova Italia" Editrice, Santa Maria degli Angeli 1989.

C. JANNELLA, *Simone Martini*, Scala, Florence 1989.

E. LUNGHI, "Una 'copia' antica dagli affreschi del Maestro di San Francesco," in *Paragone*, no. 467, 1989, pp. 12-20.

C. VOLPE, *Pietro Lorenzetti*, edited by M. Lucco, Electa, Milan 1989.

VAR. AUTHORS, *Basilica Patriarcale in Assisi. San Francesco. Testimonianza artistica. Messaggio evangelico*, Fabbri Editore, Milan 1991.

E. LUNGHI, "Per la fortuna della Basilica di S. Francesco ad Assisi: i corali domenicani della Biblioteca 'Augusta' di Perugia," in *Bollettino della Deputazione Storia Patria per l'Umbria*, LXXXVIII, 1991, pp. 43-68..

E. LUNGHI, "'Rubeus me fecit': scultura in Umbria alla fine del Duecento," in *Studi di Storia dell'Arte*, no. 2, 1991, pp. 9-32.

P. MAGRO, *La basilica sepolcrale di San Francesco in Assisi*, Casa Editrice Francescana, Assisi 1991.

W. SCHENKLUHN, *San Francesco in Assisi: Ecclesia Specialis*, Wissenschaftliche Buchgeschellschaft, Darmstadt 1991.

J. WIENER, *Die Bauskulptur von San Francesco in Assisi*, Dietrich-Coelde-Verlag, Werl/Westfalen 1991.

F. TODINI, "Un'opera romana di Giotto," in *Studi di Storia dell'Arte*, no. 3, 1992, pp. 9-22.

E. LUNGHI, "Puccio Capanna nella confraternita di S. Gregorio di Assisi," in *Arte Cristiana*, no. 754, 1993, pp. 3-14..

F. MARTIN, *Die Apsisverglasung der Oberkirche von S. Francesco in Assisi*, Wernersche Verlagsgesellschaft, Worms 1993.

S. NESSI, *La basilica di S. Francesco in Assisi e la sua documentazione storica*, Casa Editrice Francescana, Assisi 1994.

Il Gotico europeo in Italia, edited by V. Pace and M. Bagnoli, Electa, Naples 1994.

S. ROMANO, "Roma, Assisi" in *Pittura murale in Italia dal tardo Duecento ai primi del Quattrocento*, edited by M. Gregori, Edizioni Bolis, Bergamo 1995.

F. FLORES D'ARCAIS, *Giotto*, Federico Motta Editore, Milan 1995.

E. LUNGHI, *Il Crocefisso di Giunta Pisano e l'Icona del 'Maestro di San Francesco' alla Porziuncola*, Assisi 1995.

Index of Artists